2219

WF 220 / 658

WF 658 RAT

£53.95

T

# A Colour Atlas of
# Endoscopic Diagnosis in Early Stage Lung Cancer

Harubumi Kato M.D.
*Professor, Department of Surgery*
*Tokyo Medical College*

Takeshi Horai M.D.
*Chief of Clinical Research and Oncology of Lung Cancer*
*The Center for Adult Diseases, Osaka*

Translated by
J. Patrick Barron
*Professor, International Medical Communications Center*
*Tokyo Medical College*

Wolfe Publishing Ltd

WF 658 KAT

Copyright © Harubumi Kato and Takeshi Horai, 1992
Published by Wolfe Publishing Ltd, 1992
From the Japanese edition of 'Early stage lung cancer —
endoscopic findings'. © 1988, Published by: Kanehara & Co.
Ltd., Tokyo, Japan. Printed in Japan
© English text translation, Wolfe Publishing Ltd, 1992
Printed by BPCC Hazell Books Ltd, Aylesbury, England
ISBN 0 7234 1687 7

A CIP catalogue record for this book is available from the
British Library.

For full details of all Wolfe titles please write to
Wolfe Publishing Ltd, Brook House, 2–16 Torrington Place,
London WC1E 7LT, England.

# Contents

# Foreword to English Edition

This is a superb book. It is excellently written and illustrated by the leading investigators in the field of early lung cancer. It is a comprehensive review of early lung cancer, including the epidemiology, etiology, detection, localization, and treatment of the disease.

Writing a foreword to this book provides me with an opportunity to compare the lung cancer experience in Japan with that of the United States. There are many similarities between the two countries. The United States also faces an epidemic of lung cancer. Smoking is clearly related to squamous cell and small-cell carcinoma. There appears to be at least a 20-year lag between the increased use of cigarettes and the increased incidence of lung cancer in both the female and the male populations in this country. In addition, there has been a noticeable decrease in the percentage of squamous cell cancer, with a reciprocal increase in the incidence of small-cell and adenocarcinoma, over recent years; the cause of this is unclear.

In 1991, it is anticipated that there will be 161,000 new lung cancers: 101,000 in males and 60,000 in females. The estimated cancer deaths due to lung cancer are 143,000: 92,000 for males and 51,000 for females. Among males, lung cancer accounts for 19% of all cancers and is ranked second behind prostatic cancer in incidence. However, lung cancer is the leading cause of death from cancer among males (34%). In females, lung cancer is 11% of the cancers and ranks third behind breast and colorectal cancer. However, lung cancer is the leading cause of cancer death (21%).

Japanese researchers found that there is a 60% five-year survival for stage I cancer, a 30% five-year survival for stage II cancer, a 10% survival for stage III cancer, and a 5% survival for stage IV cancer. The United States' experience is similar. Cancers diagnosed at the very earliest stages, particularly centrally situated, roentgenographically occult squamous cell carcinomas have five-year survival greater than 90%. Japanese researchers report a 98% five-year survival for early central lung cancer and an 85% five-year survival for peripheral early stage cancer.

During the 1970s, there was a 10-year multicenter prospective study of the effect of screening for lung cancer using sputum cytology and chest roentgenography on lung cancer mortality. The Mayo Lung Project was one of the participating centers. Sputum cytology alone detected approximately 15% of the lung cancers. In the screened patients, more lung cancers were identified at an early stage and more of the patients were surgical candidates than in the control group. There was a higher rate of resectability in the screened group. The five-year survival for patients with lung cancer was 35% in the screened group and 15% in the control group. The increased survival was due to lead-time bias, since the cancers were diagnosed earlier than they would have been without screening.

Unfortunately, the results of this randomized trial at Mayo Clinic showed that offering both sputum cytology and chest roentgenography to high-risk outpatients every 4 months produced no mortality advantage over our standard medical practice that included recommending annual testing with these two procedures. The overall mortality from lung cancer was the same in both groups. Surprisingly, there was a higher rate of small-cell lung cancer than had been anticipated (25%); this is a cancer that is not amenable to screening nor to treatment with surgical resection. Squamous cell carcinoma, which is amenable to screening with sputum cytology and is surgically treatable, made up only one-third of the cancer cases in this study. In addition, there was a high rate of subsequent lung cancer, with significant mortality related to the next cancer. Most surprising, there were a larger number of cancers identified in the screened group (206) compared with the control group (160). Early stage squamous cell cancers did appear to have a lower mortality, but the numbers were smaller than expected and the study was not designed to specifically look at early stage squamous cell carcinoma.

The early stage lung cancer cases at Mayo Clinic have been studied thoroughly. Roentgenographically occult lung cancer is squamous cell carcinoma of the central airways: trachea, main stem bronchi, lobar bronchi and, occasionally, segmental bronchi. Roentgenographically occult lung cancer comprises approximately 15% of all lung cancers. In the Mayo Lung Project, the prevalence of roentgenographically occult squamous cell carcinoma was 17%. During the 10 years of the prospective phase of the study, the incidence was 9%. Of the roentgenographically occult lung cancers, 28% were also bronchoscopically occult. Early squamous cell carcinoma had a significant incidence of multicentricity, with 7% demonstrating simultaneous cancers and a metachronous cancer appearing at a rate of 5% per year.

Of those roentgenographically occult lung cancers visible at the time of bronchoscopy, 23% were demonstrated to have N1 nodal involvement. On the other hand, all cancers which were not bronchoscopically visible, but were within the reach of the bronchoscope and proven to exist by biopsy and brushings, were either *in situ* carcinomas or *in situ* carcinomas with microinvasion and showed no evidence of extrabronchial spread or nodal involvement.

Careful microscopic examination based on serial histologic sectioning of the resected roentgenographically occult lung cancers demonstrated that 35% of the lesions were *in situ* carcinoma, 17% demonstrated intramucosal invasion, 14% invaded to the bronchial cartilages, 17% invaded the full thickness of the bronchial wall, and 17% invaded through the bronchial wall into the extrabronchial tissue. Therefore, 83% of these cancers were confined within the full thickness of the bronchial wall.

The Mayo experience with roentgenographically occult squamous cell carcinoma demonstrates a five-year survival of 74% when all causes of deaths are included and a 90% five-year survival for death due to lung cancer alone.

Professor Kato and his colleagues make an excellent attempt to define the clinical and endoscopic criteria for diagnosing a central early stage squamous cell carcinoma. Establishing nonsurgical criteria for diagnosing early stage cancer has proven to be a difficult task. However, this is crucial if we are going to make progress in the development and evaluation of bronchoscopically-based nonsurgical treatments of early stage lung cancer. I agree with their criteria and believe that, if followed closely, the risk of mistakenly assuming that a cancer is early stage (limited to the bronchial wall and without metastases) will be very low.

This book demonstrates that detection and localization of early stage lung cancer is clearly possible. Survival after treatment for early stage cancer is greater than 90% if treated with surgical resection. However, the mortality from lung cancer is still a problem, due to the multicentric nature of the disease. Therefore, the availability of multiple treatment modalities is important in managing a patient with squamous cell lung cancer. The therapeutic modalities currently available include surgery, chemotherapy, locally administered chemotherapy, external beam radiation therapy, endobronchial radiation therapy, photodynamic therapy, and YAG laser phototherapy. It is quite common to use a combination of any of these options when treating the individual patient with squamous cell carcinoma. I extend my congratulations and encouragement to these authors in their continued work to refine these techniques for the benefit of our patients.

DENIS A. CORTESE, M.D., F.C.C.P.
*Professor, Department of Thoracic Diseases
and Internal Medicine,
Mayo Clinic, Rochester, MN 55905*

# Foreword from Japanese Edition

Early stage central lung cancer is now considered to have the same high curability by surgical treatment as early stage gastric and breast cancer.

In order to reduce the increasing mortality from lung cancer it is necessary to detect early stage cases. The government of Japan has attempted to contribute to this endeavor by including lung cancer surveys as part of the general medical care for the elderly. In these surveys, chest X-ray and sputum cytology examinations are included, the former primarily intended to detect peripheral and the latter central, early stage lung cancer.

Since early stage central lesions do not display abnormalities on the chest radiograph, sputum cytology has to be employed in their detection. Fiberoptic bronchoscopy is extremely effective in the localization of sputum cytology-positive cases.

While sputum cytology is indeed effective in the detection of early stage central lung cancer, it still involves certain problems. One of these is that there are many lung cancer cases that do not complain of sputum. Another is the difficulty of distinguishing between atypical squamous metaplastic and carcinoma cells, and in certain extremely early stage lesions it is sometimes impossible to determine their location, even by the most meticulous endoscopic procedures. To solve these problems, methods such as sputum induction, cytochemistry, and laser photodynamic localization have been developed.

As a result of these varied efforts to improve detection of lung cancer at an early stage, clinicians are routinely encountering increasing numbers of cases with normal chest radiographs.

In order to diagnose early stage lung cancer correctly, it is absolutely essential to be thoroughly familiar with the spectrum of endoscopic findings that these lesions can present.

This volume, compiled by Professor Harubumi Kato of the Department of Surgery of Tokyo Medical College and Dr. Takeshi Horai, Director of the Osaka Center for Adult Diseases, includes approximately 60 cases of early stage central lung cancer. The cases, contributed from institutions throughout Japan, are classified into groups on the basis of the endoscopic findings. The excellent endoscopic and microscopic records of these cases should be of extreme interest not only to the lung cancer specialist but also to those in general practice, medical students, and cytologists.

In addition, the cogent and extensive foreword by Professor Denis Cortese of the Department of Thoracic Diseases and Internal Medicine of the Mayo Clinic provides a valuable overview of early stage lung cancer detection in North America.

YOSHIHIRO HAYATA, M.D.
*Emeritus Professor,*
*Director, Tokyo Medical*
*College Cancer Center*

# Collaborators

Shosaku Abe — *Associate Professor, First Department of Internal Medicine, Hokkaido University.*

Yoshiro Ebihara — *Professor, Second Department of Pathology, Tokyo Medical College.*

Naganobu Hayashi — *Associate Professor, Department of Surgery, Tokyo Medical College.*

Harubumi Kato — *Professor, Department of Surgery, Tokyo Medical College.*

Norihiko Kawate — *Department of Surgery, Tokyo Medical College.*

Chimori Konaka — *Associate Professor, Department of Surgery, Tokyo Medical College.*

Hideki Shinohara — *Department of Surgery, Tokyo Medical College.*

Hiroshi Nishio — *Clinical Research and Oncology of Lung Cancer, The Center for Adult Diseases, Osaka.*

Shinichiro Nakamura — *Clinical Research and Oncology of Lung Cancer, The Center for Adult Diseases, Osaka.*

Takashi Baba — *Director, Takasaki Health Centre, Takasaki, Gunma Prefecture.*

Masahiro Fukuoka — *Director of Second Department of Internal Medicine, Osaka Prefectural Habikino Hospital.*

Kiyoyuki Furuse — *Head of First Department of Internal Medicine, National Kinki Central Hospital for Chest Diseases.*

Takeshi Horai — *Chief of Clinical Research and Oncology of Lung Cancer, The Center for Adult Diseases, Osaka.*

Shiro Makimura — *First Department of Internal Medicine, Hokkaido University.*

Hiroshi Miyamoto — *Assistant Professor, First Department of Internal Medicine, Hokkaido University.*

Kazuo Yoneyama — *Department of Surgery, Tokyo Medical College.*

# 1 Introduction

## REASONS FOR THE INCREASING OCCURRENCE OF LUNG CANCER

Lung cancer and the mortality rates for lung cancer are on the increase in almost all countries for which statistics are available (**1**).

In Japan, recent mortality rates due to malignant neoplasms have shown a slight rate of increase among males, while among females there has been a slight decrease. This can be linked to the decrease in mortality due to gastric cancer among both males and females and to the decrease in mortality due to uterine cancer in females. However, concerning mortality rates for lung cancer, the rates in 1984 were 9 times that of the rate in 1950 for males and 7.6 times for females (**1**). Today (1991), it is believed that it will be only a matter of time before the mortality rate for lung cancer exceeds that for gastric cancer.[1]

While lung cancer is on the increase in many countries, the increase in Japan is particularly acute (**2**)[2] and, if this continues to increase it is possible that in the twenty-first century Japan will earn the dubious distinction of being the country with the highest lung-cancer mortality rate in the world.[3]

### Factors in the pathogenesis of lung cancer

The mechanism of the development of lung cancer is not fully understood, yet from the particular nature of the lung it is clear that carcinogenic materials in the environment that

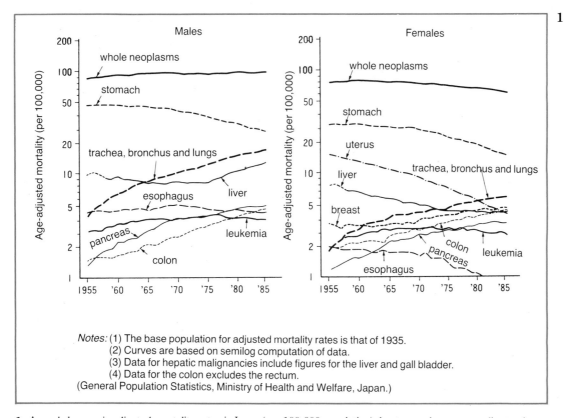

*Notes:* (1) The base population for adjusted mortality rates is that of 1935.
(2) Curves are based on semilog computation of data.
(3) Data for hepatic malignancies include figures for the liver and gall bladder.
(4) Data for the colon excludes the rectum.
(General Population Statistics, Ministry of Health and Welfare, Japan.)

**1** Annual changes in adjusted mortality rates in Japan (per 100,000 population) due to neoplasms, according to site.

come into contact with the lungs are of prime importance in this process. The main factors that have been identified so far are as follows:

- Cigarette smoke.
- Atmospheric pollution.
- Workplace carcinogens.

*Tobacco smoke*

Cigarette smoke carries the greatest relative risk for lung cancer and is the main factor responsible for the increased incidence of lung cancer. The following points have been established:

- Tobacco smoke tar contains several carcinogenic materials.
- Tobacco smoke tar causes cancer in animals.
- Heavy smokers have a high incidence of atypical metaplasia of the bronchial mucosa.
- Cigarette smoking is related to the frequency of lung cancer incidence.

The risk of cancer for smokers increases with the number of cigarettes smoked per day. According to the data of Hirayama,[4,5] if the incidence of lung cancer among non-smokers is set at 1, the incidence is 2.45 for those who smoke 1–9 cigarettes per day, 5.41 for those who

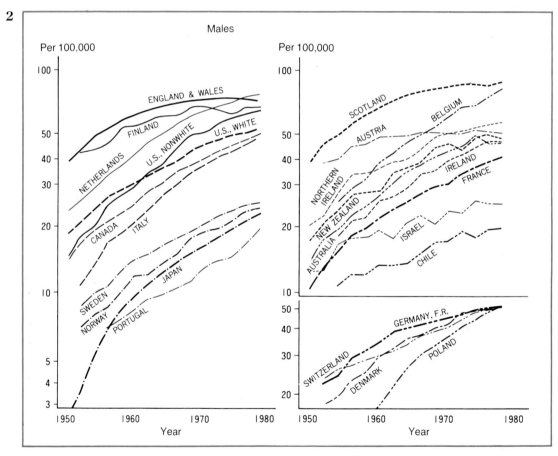

**2** Annual changes in adjusted mortality rates due to lung cancer in various countries for the period 1950–1979. (Kurihara *et al.*, 1984, *Cancer Mortality Statistics in the World*, University of Nagoya Press.)

smoke 10–19, 8.59 for those who smoke 20–39, and 15.12 for those who smoke 40 or more cigarettes per day.

The volume of cigarettes sold in Japan increased gradually from 1904, when the Tobacco Sales Monopoly Corporation was founded, until 1943, decreased temporarily during World War II, and then suddenly and rapidly increased. In other words, the spread of tobacco in Japan was later than in many Western countries, but the volume became massive after World War II.

Tobacco's carcinogenic effect is thought to begin once the cumulative amount smoked reaches a certain level. Since the number of Japanese who have reached that level has increased, this is thought to be related to the recently observed annual increase. Since cigarette smoking has been popular for a longer time in the UK and USA than in Japan, most older smokers have already accumulated a long smoking history; they show a stable mortality rate, according to the number of cigarettes smoked. Furthermore, there has been a decline in the numbers of smokers in those countries since the 1940s and recently there has been a tendency for the mortality rate to decrease.

The increasing incidence of lung cancer in women is a worldwide phenomenon. The increase in the number of female smokers and the effect of passive (indirect) smoking have been cited as the reasons. Researchers in various countries have pointed out that a non-smoking spouse of a smoker is at greater risk, depending on the number of cigarettes smoked by the other spouse, and this is thought to be one of the factors responsible for the increase in lung cancer among non-smoking women.

### The role of air pollution and workplace–related factors in the pathogenesis of lung cancer

*Air pollution.* The mortality rate for lung cancer is high in industrially advanced countries, such as the UK, USA and Germany, while it is low in developing countries, such as China, India, and Mexico. Apart from longevity, it is suggested that environmental factors, particularly air pollution, may be involved; this is reflected by the high incidence of lung cancer in the industrialized cities of Tokyo and Osaka. As many areas of Japan become more and more industrialized, the danger of increasing lung cancer related to air pollution is real. Previously, the main culprit for atmospheric pollution was factory emissions, but with increasing desulfuration, denitration, and the use of particle filters, this has changed, and now the main source of air pollutants is the automobile. Following strict anti-pollution regulations, nitrogen oxide emission by automobiles has decreased, but because the number of automobiles has increased the levels of these gases have not fallen. In addition, regulations covering diesel vehicles are not sufficiently strict; therefore, nitrogen oxides and particulate exhaust from these vehicles is a problem. It has also been shown that the nitroallene compounds contained in diesel exhaust have strong carcinogenic effects.[6]

*Carcinogens in the workplace.* Many materials, including uranium, chrome, asbestos, arsenic, beryllium, and hematite, are known carcinogens. A report in the USA revealed that there was a high incidence of lung cancer among aluminium miners, while in Japan high rates of lung cancer are seen among workers in factories that use chrome and copper. Asbestos has received special attention. With the recognition that exposure to asbestos is an everyday occurrence, many Western countries enacted strict anti-asbestos legislation; such legislation is much weaker in Japan. Since it is known that smoking can have not only additive but also synergistic effects with some of the above-mentioned carcinogens, there is increasing pressure to forbid smoking in workplaces where the use of such materials is unavoidable.

### Other carcinogens and lung cancer

Connections have been pointed out between eating large amounts of meat and fat and lung cancer; therefore, the increasing Westernization of the traditional Japanese diet may be a factor in the increasing incidence of lung cancer in the nation. A diet with a large amount of green and yellow vegetables has been linked with a decreased mortality rate for lung cancer. Green and yellow vegetables contain large amounts of ß-carotene and are major sources of vitamin A. Epidemiological studies have indicated that even in individuals with a history of smoking, a large intake of carotene is linked with a decrease in the incidence of lung cancer (especially squamous cell carcinoma and small-cell carcinoma). It would therefore seem that dietary planning has a role to play in the prevention of lung cancer.[7]

4

There are thought to be significant differences in the proliferative mechanisms of the various histologic types of lung cancer. A relationship between squamous cell and small-cell carcinomas and smoke and other chemical carcinogens has been known for some time. In adenocarcinoma, the numbers of smokers account for 1.5 times the number of non-smoking cases of this histologic type. In Japan, there have been significant increases not only in squamous cell carcinoma but also in adenocarcinoma.[8] Since many peripheral lung cancers are adenocarcinoma, it is essential to further elucidate the etiological mechanism.

## THE NEED TO DETECT EARLY STAGE LUNG CANCER

The problem of tackling the rapid increase in the mortality rate for lung cancer (**1** and **2**) is now being addressed: the government of Japan has taken the step of including surveys on lung cancer in the items covered by the Elderly Health Law.

The results of surgical treatment of lung cancer vary according to the stage of the disease. A multi-institution survey by the Ohta Research Group of the Cancer Research Fund of the Ministry of Health and Welfare (1982) indicated that the 5-year survival rate of stage I cases was approximately 60%, that of stage II 30%, stage III 10%, and stage IV 5% (**3**). It is only natural that the earlier the stage of disease the better the results of treatment would be, and the results of treatment of early stage lung cancer cases are relatively good. At present the 5-year survival rate of central early stage lung cancer is approximately 100%, while that for peripheral early stage lung cancer is approximately 85% (*see* Chapter 4). Therefore, to decrease the mortality rate for lung cancer the importance of detection at the early stage cannot be over-emphasized.

### Lung cancer surveys

In the United States, experimental surveys were carried out in the 1970s to determine the effectiveness of mass screening programs in the treatment of lung cancer. Large-scale programs were undertaken at the Mayo Clinic, the Sloan-Kettering Cancer Center and the Johns Hopkins Hospital. In particular, the Mayo Clinic project sought to determine whether there would be any benefit from adding sputum cytology to regular chest radiographic examinations. Although an increase in the detection of lung cancer, including early stage lung cancer, was demonstrated in these programs, there was no decrease in lung cancer mortality. It was concluded that such mass surveys were not cost effective and as a result they were discontinued.[9]

Despite the negative image of lung cancer mass surveys in the United States, in Japan such surveys are carried out with public funding. It has been shown that, as a result, a greater number of early stage lung cancer cases are detected and, indeed, many people owe their continuing lives to early detection and treatment. Nevertheless, since none of these projects were prospective randomized studies, it is extremely difficult to demonstrate a statistically significant difference from controls. In the US surveys, it was extremely difficult to obtain statistically significant results. In Japan, however, we proceeded with studies, ethically designed, with controls, and with meticulous record-keeping and follow-up.

Mass chest radiographic surveys commenced in Japan in the early 1950s, originally for the detection of pulmonary tuberculosis, but as they progressed, lung cancer became the primary focus of interest. It became apparent that this was an effective method for the detection of peripheral lung cancer. Twenty years later, sputum cytology was added experimentally for high-risk cases. It was found to be effective in the detection of central lung cancer. Therefore, a combination of chest radiograph and sputum cytology would be ideal for screening for lung cancer. However, the costs involved in combined surveys are high, albeit justifiable, and there are also the problems of training radiologists, developing reading systems, training competent cytology screeners and maintaining quality screening.

There are already many lung cancer screening systems in Japan, some operating at the local or municipal level, some at the workplace, and health check-up institutions. There are also public service health education television broadcasts which encourage viewers in the high-risk group or with symptoms to write or phone for a sputum cytology kit that can be mailed to the screening center. Furthermore, under the provisions of the Elderly Health Act, all those aged 40 or over are entitled to a free chest radiograph, and those aged 50 or over, with a smoking index (number of cigarettes per day × number of years smoked) of 600 or more, or with symptoms such as bloody sputum (high-risk group), are also entitled to a sputum cytology examination.

## Detection and increase of central early stage lung cancer

With the spread of screening projects the number of early stage lung cancers being detected has also increased. At the Department of Surgery of Tokyo Medical College, 3,106 cases of lung cancer had been treated by July 1987, among which there were 146 cases (4.7%) of early stage lung cancer. Taking 1980, the approximate date when sputum cytology began to be aggressively pursued, as a base, it can be seen that before 1980 early stage cases accounted for 3.7% of cases, whereas after 1980 they accounted for 5.8% (4).

In most of the early stage central cases of lung cancer detected by sputum cytology, there are no abnormal radiographic findings and fiberoptic bronchoscopy is essential for localization of the lesion. However, among the cases of lung cancer that are detected by sputum cytology there are some extremely early stage lesions in which the lesion cannot be determined even by bronchoscopy. Such cases must be followed up with great care until the site of the lesion can be determined.

The number of roentgenologically occult early stage cases detected by sputum cytology in the 5-year period before the introduction of sputum cytology as a *screening* method in 1974 was only 1 or 2; the number increased to 5 in the 5-year period from 1975–1979, jumped to 29 cases in 1980–1984, and reached 31 in the period 1985–1989 (5). Thus, the detection of early stage lung

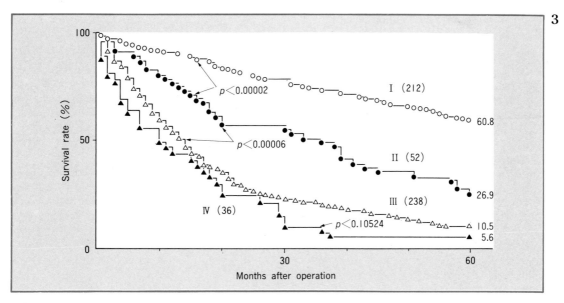

3

**3** Prognosis of lung cancer. (Based on data from seven representative institutions in the Ohta Research Group, funded by the Cancer Research Fund of the Ministry of Health and Welfare.)

cancer has increased as a result of sputum cytology screening.

## WHAT IS CENTRAL EARLY STAGE LUNG CANCER?

Early stage lung cancer should consist of those lung cancers which can be diagnosed clinically and which can be curatively treated. The structure of the lung shows transition from relatively large airways to peripheral alveoli and the process of proliferation of different histologic types of lung cancer also shows variation. In 1965, Hattori[10] proposed that lesions limited to the bronchial wall in larger bronchi as far as subsegmental bronchi, as shown in **6**, should be considered as central lung cancer. Subsequently, discussion among the Ikeda Research Group of the Ministry of Health and Welfare Cancer Research Fund proposed the following definition of hilar carcinoma:[11]

The definition of hilar early stage lung cancer should be based on pathological examination of the resected specimen, and the lesion should:

- Originate from large bronchi as far as segmental bronchi.
- Be limited to the bronchial wall.
- Have no lymph node or distant metastasis.
- Be any histologic type of lung cancer.

As a result of progress in fiberoptic bronchoscopy it became possible to visualize lesions peripheral to subsegmental bronchi and it also became possible to detect lesions in such areas which were limited to the bronchial wall and in which there was no metastasis. Furthermore, with the development of non-surgical therapeutic methods, such as photodynamic therapy, it was not always possible to have a resected specimen to examine following the therapeutic procedure. Therefore, the lesions fitting the definition of early stage central lung cancer actually increased. The early stage lung cancers presented in this book are primarily those in which fiberoptic examination was possible, and since most of these are squamous cell carcinomas, the focus of this book is on that histologic type of lung cancer.

## HISTOPATHOLOGICAL FEATURES

The macroscopic appearance of biopsied or resected specimens of early stage lung cancer suggest thickening or swelling of the mucosa, with granularity or nodularity. One of the features of this entity is that it is not accompanied by necrosis. In particular, in intraepithelial cancer (carcinoma *in situ*) there is only mild swelling or thickening, and in certain areas it is almost impossible to make a distinction from normal tissue. It is therefore extremely important to keep these points in mind when preparing biopsy or resected specimens.

### Histological findings

Intraepithelial carcinoma (carcinoma *in situ*) is the most appropriate entity for consideration as early stage cancer. Histologically, such cases show squamous cell carcinoma cells of abnormal structure, but the findings are limited to within the epithelium.[12] There is a significant variation, however, in the interpretation of findings depending on the individual pathologist. There is not yet as strong a consensus as in the case of the histological findings of *in situ* carcinoma of the uterine cervix. Findings of the same degree of atypia have been reported as indicating severe atypia[12–14] or as carcinoma *in situ*.[15,16] According to the definition of intraepithelial carcinoma, the basement membrane below the lesion should be preserved. In cases in which the inferior portion of the abnormal epithelium shows a wave-like configuration (**7** and **8**), the basement membrane has been destroyed and the lesion is in the early invasive stage.

The normal basement membrane can appear relatively thick, indicating that it is well preserved, whereas in some cases with abnormal epithelium the basement membrane appears unclear or disrupted (**9**, **10** and **11**), and these findings suggest invasive proliferation of the atypical epithelium.

The macroscopic appearance of central early stage lung cancer includes thickening and granularity. Histologically, squamous cell carcinoma of the lung can generally be divided into two major types:

- Basal cell type (**7** and **12**).
- Differentiated type (**13**).

Some cases, however, can resemble large cell carcinoma.

In the basal cell type the layer of malignant cells becomes thinner as it extends under the ciliated epithelium, at which sites making a

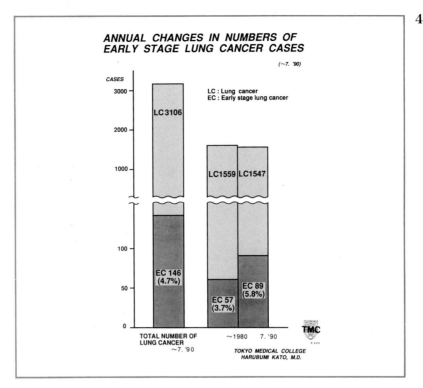

**4** Annual changes in numbers of early stage lung cancer cases. (Department of Surgery, Tokyo Medical College, 1950 – July 1990.)

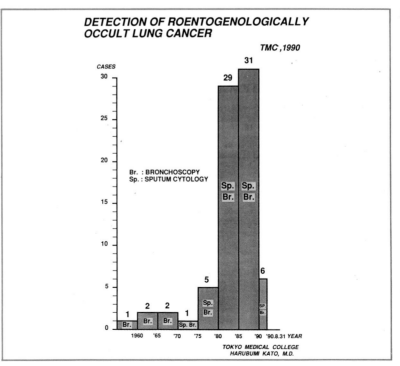

**5** Annual changes in the detection of radiologically occult early stage lung cancer. (Department of Surgery, Tokyo Medical College.)

8

6

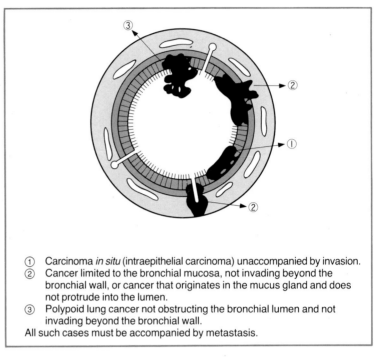

① Carcinoma *in situ* (intraepithelial carcinoma) unaccompanied by invasion.
② Cancer limited to the bronchial mucosa, not invading beyond the bronchial wall, or cancer that originates in the mucus gland and does not protrude into the lumen.
③ Polypoid lung cancer not obstructing the bronchial lumen and not invading beyond the bronchial wall.
All such cases must be accompanied by metastasis.

**6** Early stage lung cancer originating in bronchi with cartilage. (From Hattori *et al.*[10])

distinction from proliferation of basal cells or severe atypia can be extremely difficult (**10** and **14**). In the differentiated type (**9**), distinction from severe atypia can be difficult. In such cases it is important to rely on other indicators of malignancy in addition to severe atypia, such as extremely high cell density, abnormal mitotic figures, extreme disorder and keratotic cells, but it is also important to remember that not all of these features are present in all cases.

One type of development of a bronchial wall lesion involves proliferation of cancer cells along the inside of the basement membrane of the bronchial gland duct (**15**). This can be a preliminary step in development to the next stage of invasion, to the bronchial adventitia and lung parenchyma. The more marked the invasion from the deep layer of the bronchial wall to the adventitia, the more opportunities cancer cells have of invading lymph and blood vessels. There are reports[17-19] of approximately 10 cases of cancer limited to the bronchial wall with distant metastases, and most of those involved invasion to the deep layer of the bronchial wall.

**Precancerous changes**

The concept that various types of atypia occurring in the bronchi of heavy smokers develop into intraepithelial carcinoma and then invasive cancer has been suggested, and attendant upon this is the question of precancerous changes.[13,14,17,20]

This concept has also been supported by animal experiments and studies on nuclear DNA in exfoliated atypical cells by Feulgen staining in which aneuploidy becomes more distinct as the degree of metaplastic atypia advances. Since the histograms of moderate and severe metaplasia and intraepithelial carcinoma do not display significant differences, it is thought that atypia may already possess characteristics of malignancy.[21,22] On the other hand, since most intraepithelial carcinoma lesions are not found associated with intraepithelial carcinoma, there is

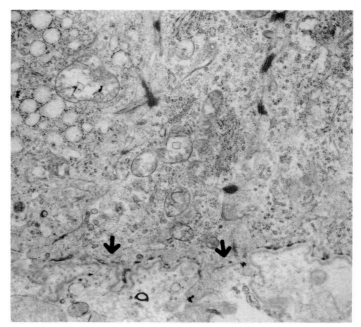

**7**

7 Wave-like formation of the basal portion. The original basement membrane cannot be identified. These findings suggest microinvasion (×200).

**8**

8 Electron microscopy of the basement membrane (thought on the basis of histological findings to be intraepithelial carcinoma). Rupture of the basement membrane can be seen (arrows) and the bundles of collagen fibers normally below the basement membrane have disappeared (×10000).

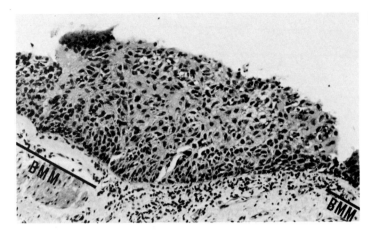

**9** Differentiated intraepithelial carcinoma that is difficult to distinguish from severely atypical squamous cell metaplasia. The basement membrane is unclear in one part. BMM indicates the areas in which the presence of the basement membrane can be recognized (×*100*).

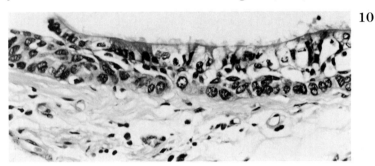

**10** Lateral extension of intraepithelial carcinoma. The area of malignancy is difficult to distinguish from proliferation of atypical basal cells. The basement membrane is unclear (×*200*).

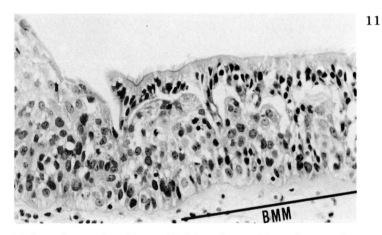

**11** Lateral extension of intraepithelial carcinoma. The malignant cells burrow under the ciliated epithelium. At its most forward extent, the basement membrane is still preserved. BMM indicates the areas in which the presence of the basement membrane can be recognized. (×*200*).

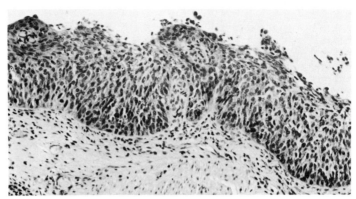

**12** Typical histological findings of intraepithelial carcinoma. All layers of the epithelium have been replaced by small cells with densely staining oval nuclei. The basal portion of the epithelium is smooth but the normal bronchial basement membrane has disappeared (×*100*).

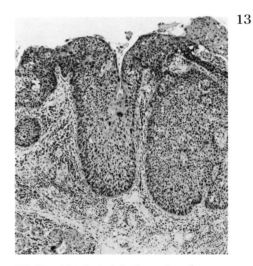

**13** The histological findings of early stage lung cancer. The thickened portion of the membrane shows differentiated squamous cell carcinoma. At the deepest portion it extends as far as the bronchial glands (×*40*).

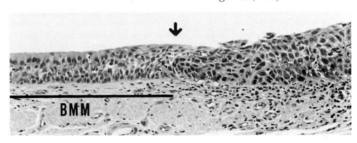

**14** The histological findings of squamous cell early stage lung cancer. The lateral extent of intraepithelial carcinoma forms a distinct border (arrow) with benign epithelium. BMM indicates the areas in which the presence of the basement membrane can be recognized. (×*100*).

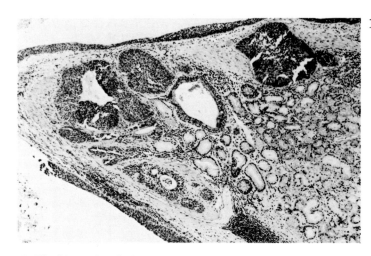

**15** The histological findings of squamous cell early stage lung cancer. The membrane is replaced by intraepithelial carcinoma and invasion to within the glandular duct is recognized (×*40*).

also the theory of *de novo* appearance of carcinoma *in situ*.[16, 23]

### Depth of cancer invasion

**Table 1** gives a breakdown of 10 resected central early stage lung cancers and two advanced cancers in which the primary lesion was less than 1.5 cm in maximum dimension. The table can be analyzed as follows:

- Four cases of intraepithelial carcinoma in which there was no clear interstitial invasion and the intraductal invasion did not extend beyond the cartilage ring.
- Four cases of microinvasive cancer in which there was intraductal or interstitial invasion that did not extend beyond the cartilage ring.
- Two cases in which invasion extended beyond the cartilage ring but not beyond the adventitia.
- Two advanced cases in which invasion extended beyond the cartilage ring and also into the parenchyma.

In the two advanced cases in which invasion into the parenchyma occurred, there was invasion into lymph or blood vessels, and one of the cases was accompanied by lymph node metastasis. Of the cases in which the lesion did not show parenchymal invasion, none showed lymph node metastasis.

Although many lung cancers larger than 1 cm or large enough to obstruct a bronchus are frequently accompanied by extramural invasion, lymphatic invasion and lymph node metastasis, there are still relatively few reports on these findings. If further progress makes it possible to correctly estimate the extent of invasion clinically, it should be possible to select more appropriate therapeutic methods for each case.

There were three cases of severe atypia in which it was extremely difficult to distinguish them from areas of cancer, but on close examination they were found to be separated by areas of normal epithelium. In four cases, the intraepithelial carcinomas neighbored mild-to-moderate atypia accompanied by proliferation of basal cells or atypia but in both of these conditions there was a significant difference in terms of cell atypia.

Further histological studies with increased numbers of cases are necessary to elucidate the origin and development of early stage lung cancer.

**Table 1.** Breakdown of central lung cancers categorized endoscopically as early stage

| Case | Age | Sex | Site | Size (cm) | Macroscopic finding | Histological type | Extent of invasion | Lymph node metastasis | Area surrounding the tumor |
|---|---|---|---|---|---|---|---|---|---|
| 1 | 54 | M | Left $B^6$ | $0.3 \times 0.6$ | Mucosal thickening | Well differentiated | Bronchial gland Upper layer of lamina propia | — | Submucosal invasion Severely atypical metaplasia |
| 2 | 62 | M | Bif. left upper/ lower div. | $0.5 \times 1$ | Mucosal thickening | Moderately differentiated | Intraepithelial | — | Submucosal invasion Severely atypical metaplasia |
| 3 | 61 | F | Right $B^6$ | $0.5 \times 0.5$ | Mucosal thickening | Poorly–moderately differentiated | Bronchial gland Upper layer of lamina propia | — | Submucosal invasion |
| 4 | 58 | F | Left $B^{1+2}$ | $0.1 \times 0.1$ | Polypoid | Moderately differentiated | Intraepithelial | — | Submucosal invasion Squamous metaplasia (mild) |
| 5 | 59 | M | Right $B^6$ | $0.5 \times 0.4$ | Mucosal thickening | Poorly differentiated | Upper layer of lamina propia | — | Submucosal invasion |
| 6 | 64 | M | Left $B_{ab}^{1+2}$ –$B^3$ | $1 \times 1$ | Mucosal thickening – granular type | Well differentiated | Upper layer of lamina propia | — | Moderate–severe atypical |
| 7 | 76 | M | Bif. left upper div./ ling. bronchi | $1 \times 1$ | Mucosal thickening | Well differentiated | Bronchial gland Upper layer of lamina propia | — | Submucosal invasion Moderately atypical Basal cell hyperplasia |
| 8 | 74 | M | Right $B^6$ Bifurcation | $1.5 \times 1.5$ | Mucosal thickening | Poorly–moderately differentiated | Bronchial gland Upper layer of lamina propia | — | Submucosal invasion Basal cell hyperplasia (moderate) |
| 9 | 75 | M | Left main-upper lobe bronchus | $3 \times 1$ | Mucosal thickening | Well differentiated | Bronchial gland Tunica adventitia | — | Submucosal invasion |
| 10 | 81 | M | Right middle lobe bronchus | $0.5 \times 0.5$ | Mucosal thickening | Poorly differentiated | Bronchial gland Tunica adventitia | — | Submucosal invasion |
| 11 | 60 | M | Right $B_a^5$ | $0.3 \times 0.2 \times 1.5$ | Mucosal thickening – polypoid | Poorly differentiated | Lung parenchyma | Lymph duct | |
| 12 | 51 | M | Left $B_c^{1+2}$ | 1.5 long-axis direction | Stenotic lumen | Poorly differentiated | Lung parenchyma | Multiple | Carcinoma *in situ* |

Cases 1–8, intraepithelial cancer; cases 5–8 accompanied by microinvasion; cases 9 and 10, early invasive cancer; cases 11 and 12, advanced cancers.

14

# REFERENCES

[1]*National Health Trends* (1986), **33**(9).

[2]Aoki, K. and Hamajima, N. (1985), The factors of occurrence in lung cancer, *Naika MOOK*, **29**, 41–50.

[3]Kuroishi, T. and Tominaga, H. (1984), Recent features of cancer mortality in Japan, *Modern Medicine*, **10**, 32–36.

[4]Hirayama, T. (1987), Smoking and lung cancer, *Diagnosis and Treatment*, **4**, 903–907.

[5]Hirayama, T. (1984), *Prevention of Cancer*, Shinjuku Shobo.

[6]Takemoto, K. (1987), Air pollution and lung cancer, *Diagnosis and Treatment*, **4**, 908–911.

[7]Kvale, G., Bjelke, E. and Gart, J. J. (1983), Dietary habits and lung cancer risk, *Int. J. Cancer*, **31**, 397–405.

[8]Shimizu, H. (1981), Comparisons of lung cancer incidence rates between Japan and U.S.A. by sex and histologic type, *Lung Cancer*, **21**, 519–524.

[9]American Cancer Society (1980), *ACS Report on the Cancer Related Health Checkup*, pp. 6–12.

[10]Hattori, S., Matsuda, M. *et al.* (1965), Early detection of lung cancer, *Igaku-Shoin*, **2**.

[11]Ikeda, S. (1976), Atlas of early lung cancer in the hilum, *Igaku-Shoin*, 2–3.

[12]Woolner, L. B. (1986), *Lung in the Pathology of Incipient Neoplasia*, W. B. Saunders, pp. 57–85.

[13]Dunbill, M S. (1987), Carcinoma of the bronchus and lung. In *Pulmonary Pathology,* Churchill Livingstone, London, pp. 333–401.

[14]Nasiell, M. and Kato, H. (1987), Cytological studies in man and animals on development of bronchogenic carcinoma. In *Lung Carcinomas*, ed. by E. M. McDowell, Churchill Livingstone, London, pp. 207–242.

[15]Carter, D. and Egglestone, J. C. (1980), Squamous cell carcinoma. In *Atlas of Tumor Pathology: Tumors of the Lower Respiratory Tract,* AFIP, 70–94.

[16]Suemasu, K., Shimosato, Y. *et al.* (1974), Multiple minute cancers of major bronchi, *J. Thorac. Cardiovasc. Surg.*, **68**, 664–672.

[17]Carter, D. *et al.*(1976), Relationships of morphology to clinical presentation in ten cases of early squamous cell carcinoma of the lung, *Cancer,* **37**, 1389–1396.

[18]Mason, M. K. and Jordan, J. W. (1982), Outcome of carcinoma *in situ* and early invasive carcinoma of the bronchus, *Thorax*, **37**, 453–456.

[19]Tao, L. C., Chamberlain, D. W., Delarue, N. C., Pearson, F. G. and Donat, E. E. (1982), Cytologic diagnosis of radiographically occult squamous cell carcinoma of the lung, *Cancer*, **50**, 1580–1586.

[20]Saccomanno, G. *et al.* (1974), Development of carcinoma of the lung as reflected in exfoliated cells, *Cancer*, **33**, 256–270.

[21]Nasiell, M., Kato, H. *et al.* (1978), Cancer. Cytomorphological grading and Feulgen DNA analysis of metaplastic and neoplastic bronchial cells, *Cancer,* **41**, 1511–1521.

[22]Kato, H., Konaka, C. *et al.* (1983), *Cytology of the Lung*, Igaku-Shoin, Tokyo.

[23]Melamed, M. R., Zaman, M. B. *et al.* (1977), Radiologically occult *in situ* and incipient invasive epidermoid lung cancer, *Am. J. Surg. Pathol.*, **1**, 5–16.

# 2 Methods of Detection

With progress in the interpretation of radiographs and in fiberoptic bronchoscopy, the number of cases of lung cancer that are detected at an early stage is increasing. As mentioned in Chapter 1, with increasing acceptance of sputum cytology, the numbers of early stage lesions detected in large bronchi (i.e. central or hilar lung cancers), in particular, have shown an increase in recent years. Morphologically, central early stage lung cancers display different types of growth and development – as polyps, invasive nodules or as superficial invasion[1] – and there are also intra-epithelial carcinomas *in situ* that have not extended beyond the basement membrane (**16**). Because such small early stage lesions are limited to the bronchial lumen they frequently evince no abnormality on plain chest radiographs; therefore, sputum cytology plays an important role in their detection.

Of the 44 early stage central lung cancers we

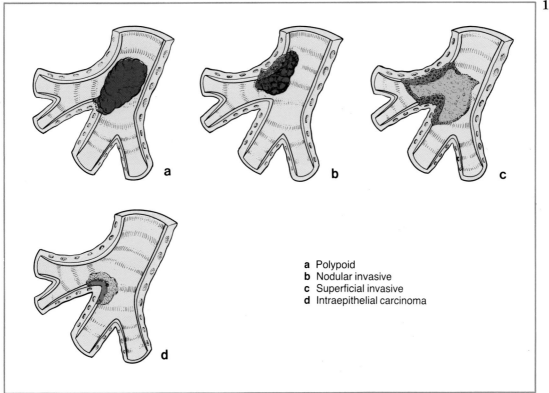

**16**

**a** Polypoid
**b** Nodular invasive
**c** Superficial invasive
**d** Intraepithelial carcinoma

**16** Types of development of central early stage lung cancer.

**Table 2.** Results of chest radiographs and central early stage lung cancer (cord-like shadow). (Center for Adult Diseases, Osaka, 1987.)

| | Number of cases | Chest radiography findings | | Positive rate (%) for sputum cytology |
| --- | --- | --- | --- | --- |
| | | − | + | |
| Intraepithelial carcinoma | 5 | 5 | 0 | 5/5 (100) |
| Superficial invasion | 13 | 11 | 2 | 11/13 (85) |
| Nodular invasion | 9 | 6 | 3 | 8/8 (100) |
| Polyp | 13 | 5 | 8 | 8/12 (66) |
| Mixed | 1 | 0 | 1 | 1/1 (100) |
| Multiple | 3 | 2 | 1 | 3/3 (100) |

examined (**Table 2**), 29 showed no abnormality whatsoever on the chest radiograph and were detected by sputum cytology. In the polypoid growths, which are sometimes detected on the basis of secondary changes, the positive rate for sputum cytology was slightly poorer than for other growth types.

## SYMPTOMS AND REASONS FOR DETECTION

Even for a small lesion, if it is located in a large airway the patient can experience cough, sputum or bloody sputum, which is the most striking symptom of central early stage lung cancer. The appearance of bloody sputum, however, is probably a strong stimulus for the patient to undergo a health check and a more typical pattern would be a long-term productive cough. If a large bronchus becomes obstructed, the patient experiences dyspnea, respiratory distress, or asthma-like attacks. If the pulmonary lobe distal to the site of obstruction becomes infected then pneumonia and fever ensue and a pneumonia-like shadow can be detected as a secondary change on the radiograph. While many cases are detected with the increasingly common mass surveys, including sputum cytology, this is not to say that

**17**

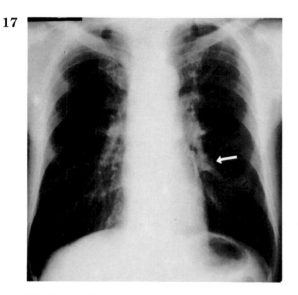

**17** Chest radiograph of central early stage lung cancer (cord-like shadow). A cord-like shadow appears as a loss of radiolucency in the left lower lobe.

**18**

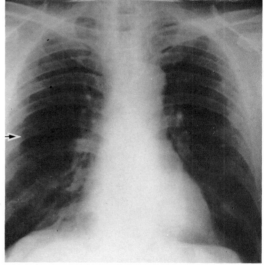

**18** Chest radiograph of central early stage lung cancer (emphysema). Increased radiolucency can be seen in the right middle lung field due to localized emphysema that results from a tumor at the orifice of right $S^6$.

19 20

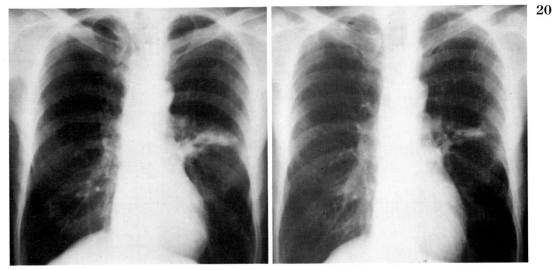

**19, 20** Chest radiograph of central early stage lung cancer (pneumonia): obstructive pneumonia shadow in left S³ (**19**); reduction of the shadow after treatment with antibiotics (**20**).

21

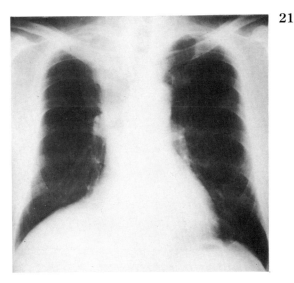

**21** Chest radiograph of central early stage lung cancer (atelectasis), showing atelectasis of the right upper lobe.

all cases detected by such screenings are asymptomatic. Especially among elderly heavy smokers, many are not particularly aware of cough or sputum, and it is exactly because of the production of sputum in such cases that detection can be made by sputum cytology.

## CHEST RADIOGRAPHS

The roentgenological findings in central early stage lung cancer include a normal appearance, cord-like or pneumonia-like shadow, atelectasis or emphysematous shadow.[2]

Since the lesion is limited to within the bronchial

**22**                                                                                                       **23**

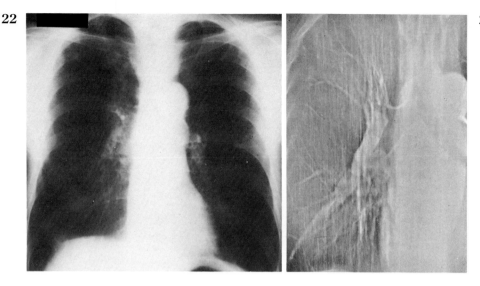

**22, 23** Chest radiograph of central early stage lung cancer (tumor): plain chest radiograph (**22**); xerotomography reveals a tumor at the orifice of the right lower lobe bronchus (**23**).

wall in cases of extremely small lesions, it is impossible to detect shadows suggestive of a tumor or invasive proliferation. Such cases with a completely normal radiographic appearance are referred to as radiologically occult lung cancer.

In the case of lesions that protrude into the bronchial lumen, the radiological appearance can vary. If there is even a slight degree of stenosis then secondary changes can be recognized. In other words, secretions accumulate distal to the lesion, the bronchus loses its radiolucency, and appears as a cord-like shadow (**17**). It is also possible for the lesion to obstruct a bronchus and act as a check valve; this causes localized emphysema distal to the lesion and results in heightened radiolucency of the lung (**18**). If the lesion is in a main bronchus the radiolucency of the right and left lungs can differ. These findings can be extremely subtle and difficult to detect, but when examining radiographs one should be keenly aware that these are possible manifestations of lung cancer.

When secretions accumulate distal to the lesion as a result of obstruction, infection and vascular engorgement are followed by pneumonia, with radiographic findings showing conditions suggestive of that condition (obstructive pneumonia), and fever. Even if the patient responds to antibiotics and the shadow is resolved (**19** and **20**) one still cannot exclude the possibility of lung cancer. Particularly in cases in which pneumonia recurs in the same site, one should aggressively follow up the possibility of lung cancer.

If the lesion completely obstructs a bronchus, air is prevented from reaching the distal area of the lung and atelectasis develops (**21**).

If a tumor protrudes into the bronchial lumen it can sometimes be demonstrated by tomography or xerotomography, even when it is not apparent on plain chest radiography (**22** and **23**).

**24**

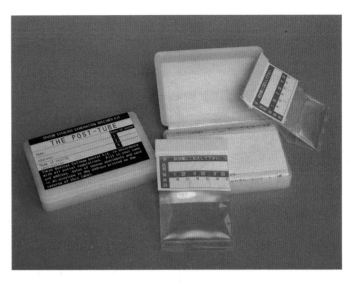

**24** Sputum cytology kit for mailing to clinical laboratories (Tokyo Medical College post tube).

## SPUTUM CYTOLOGY

Sputum cytology, a relatively simple examination procedure whereby exfoliated cancer cells are sought for among expectorated sputum specimens, does not represent a significant burden for the patient and can be repeated easily; it is essential for patients with bloody sputum or a long history of productive cough. Particularly in cases of central early stage lung cancer with no particular roentgenological abnormalities, sputum cytology is the only method of detection. The positive rate for sputum cytology for cancer patients presenting for the first time is slightly less than 40% for single-day expectorations, but rises to almost 60% for 3-day pooled specimens,

while the corresponding rates for squamous cell carcinoma as a whole are 51% and 72%, respectively, and those for central early stage lung cancer are 52% and 77%, respectively (**Table 3**). Therefore pooled specimens of at least 3 days are recommended.

### Sputum cytology – method

Examinations for sputum cytology employ either specimens smeared directly onto the slide or else the pooled specimen method in which cellular elements are extracted from the liquefied specimen. In the latter method, there is denser accumulation of cellular elements on the slide and this increases the detection rate.[3] In general

**Table 3.** Positive rates for sputum cytology according to number of examinations and site of lesion. (Center for Adult Diseases, Osaka.)

|  | *Number of cases* | *1 time (%)* | *2 times (%)* | *≥ 3 times (%)* |
|---|---|---|---|---|
| Total lung cancer | 2408 | 923 (38.3) | 1193 (49.5) | 1395 (57.9) |
| Central lung cancer | 922 | 411 (44.6) | 526 (57.0) | 602 (65.3) |
| Squamous cell carcinoma | 854 | 435 (50.9) | 533 (62.4) | 618 (72.3) |
| Early central lung cancer | 31[a] | 16 (51.6) | 23 (74.2) | 24 (77.4) |

[a]Excluding the 3-day pooled sputum method.

**25** Sputum cytology kit (post sampler): (a) container with mucolytic preservative fluid; (b) immediately after expectoration of sputum into the container; (c) 1 day later, mucus has dissolved and cellular components have sedimented; (d) the preservative fluid is discarded and the cellular components are harvested. (Matsunami Glass Co., Osaka.)

clinical practice, some of the expectorated sputum is usually smeared directly onto a slide to prepare a fresh specimen. In mass surveys, because of the numbers involved, pooled specimens, in which sputum from 3 days is pooled in preservative fluid, are usually employed.

### Direct smears of fresh sputum

Sputum produced on awakening is usually most diagnostic. To prevent the sputum drying and cells degenerating, it should be brought to the clinical laboratory as quickly as possible and the specimens prepared that day. First, the specimens are macroscopically examined; then, avoiding areas of obvious saliva, forceps are used to pick up small mounds of bloody sputum or mucus, which are placed on a glass slide; then, by pressing the specimen lightly with another glass slide it is smeared between the two slides, ensuring even distribution of the material. Once it has been smeared, the specimen should be fixed immediately for more than 30 min in a fixative, such as 95% alcohol, to prevent changes due to drying.

### Sputum preservation

*Saccomanno method.* Sputum from 3 days is pooled in sputum preservative liquid, consisting of 50% ethanol and 2% polyethylene glycol 1,540, mixed in a special blender to separate the mucus, and then centrifuged to obtain the cellular components.[4] This method has been employed mainly in mass screening projects. Cleansing of the mixer vessel can be troublesome with this method, and the number of specimens that can be prepared in a given time is limited. Also, malignant cells may be embedded in debris created by this treatment, which causes difficulties in screening, requiring a long time for microscopic examination.

*Tokyo Medical College postal specimen method.* Devised for collecting specimens sent by mail, a small plastic box, $9.5 \times 6.0 \times 1.6\,\text{cm}^3$, contains a sealable transparent vinyl pouch filled with preservative fluid (50% ethanol, Carbowax, and 1% thymol) (**24**).[5] The subject pools early morning sputum from 3 consecutive days in the pouch, seals the pouch, and places it in the box, which in turn is placed in an envelope and mailed to the examination center. Specimens are prepared at the clinical laboratory by the direct smear method described above.

*Sputum mucolytic method.* This method involves the addition of a liquid to the specimen in preservative fluid in order to dissolve the mucus of the specimen and to recover a greater amount of cellular components, thereby increasing the diagnostic accuracy. The first practical method of this type was the acetylcysteine pooled sputum method developed by one of the authors [T.H.].[3] This method was further modified to enable the handling of large numbers of mass screening specimens and it became easier to recover relatively large quantities of cellular material without complicated treatment.

In the dithiothreitol (DTT) pooled sputum method[6] the mucolytic agent dithiothreitol is added to the preservative fluid in a plastic test tube with a conical bottom in order to facilitate the sedimentation of the cellular components (**25**). When the specimen tubes are collected, the mucus is already dissolved and all that needs to be done is to discard the supernatant and prepare the specimen. The amount of time and energy required for this method is significantly less than for the Saccomanno method; therefore, a large number of specimens can be prepared in a short time. Since the specimens prepared with

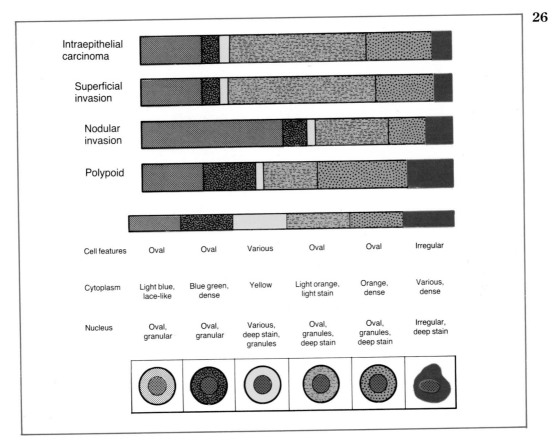

**26** Types of development of central early stage lung cancer, cytology, and the rate of detection.

**27**

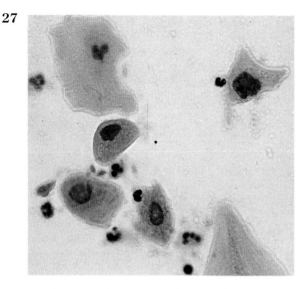

**27** Cytology of central early stage lung cancer. Keratinized cells are frequently seen in superficial invasion lesions (×*400*).

**28**

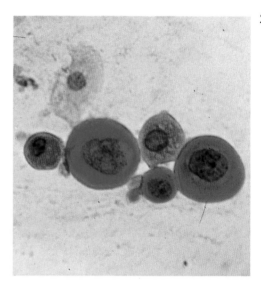

**28** Cytology of central early stage lung cancer. In nodular invasion lesions, many basal-type cells stain with light green (×*400*).

**29**

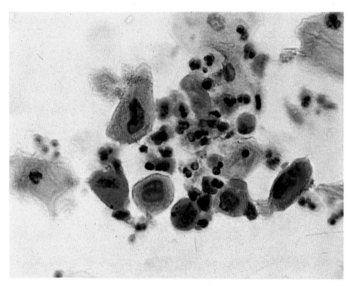

**29** Cytology of central early stage lung cancer. In polypoid lesions, cells with marked atypia and necrotic material are visible (×*400*).

this method do not have background mucus, and cellular components are evenly distributed, screening is easy: not only is the detection rate increased but also the malignant cells can appear in clusters. There is also a slim (about 3 cm) sample tube that can be used for mailing.

*Papanicolaou staining method*
The most commonly employed staining method in cytology for lung cancer is the Papanicolaou method. If the specimen dries in the course of preparation, this staining method can lead to misinterpretation. Therefore, the smeared

specimen should be placed in fixative solution immediately.

Fixation hardens the cells, prevents autolysis, and preserves the structure; for Papanicolaou staining, equal amounts of 95% ethanol and ether are used. There are other spray-type coating fixation methods (isopropanol and polyethylene glycol) and in performing these methods the prepared specimens should be immediately sprayed evenly to prevent drying.

In the Papanicolaou stain, the cell nucleus is stained by hematoxylin while the cytoplasm is stained by a combination of three acid pigments with different molecular weights (orange G, eosin, and light green). In keratotic cells, keratohyalin is present and, because the cytoplasm is compact, it is stained with the lower-molecular-weight orange G and eosin; in non-keratotic cells or cells without keratin, the cytoplasm is dense and is therefore stained by the high-molecular-weight light green. In addition to these differences in staining of the cytoplasm, the nuclear chromatin is also clearly shown and since the degree of transparency is high, observation is possible even in overlapping cells.

## Cytology of early stage squamous cell carcinoma

Almost all early stage lung cancer lesions in large airways are squamous cell carcinomas. The cells of early stage lesions that appear in sputum are not necessarily different from those of advanced cases of squamous cell carcinoma, but their numbers in the specimen are fewer, which reflects that the size of the lesion is smaller and the appearance of extremely atypical malignant cells is less frequent.

The cytological appearance of early stage squamous cell carcinoma is generally characterized by superficial keratinized cells and basal cells with limited atypia, but in practice various types of malignant cells can appear and the frequency also varies according to the growth pattern of the lesion (**26**).

In intraepithelial carcinoma or superficially invasive lesions, many malignant cells stain lightly with orange G and show only limited atypia; there are relatively few basal malignant cells staining light green (**27**). In the nodular invasion lesions, the number of basal cells staining light green increases (**28**). In the polypoid lesions, many keratotic cells stain strongly with orange G and also show marked atypia. Occasionally, necrotic materials are encountered (**29**).

When the degree of cellular atypia is marked and the cells fully satisfy the conditions for a diagnosis of malignancy, there is no problem, but in early stage squamous cell carcinoma, the number of malignant cells that appears is low and in most such cells the degree of atypia is not so marked. It can be difficult to distinguish cells of squamous cell carcinoma with a low degree of

**Table 4.** Criteria for evaluating sputum cytology mass surveys and responses made in relation to results[7,8]

| Diagnostic classification | Findings | Responses |
| --- | --- | --- |
| A | No histiocytes in the sputum | Insufficient material; repeat examination |
| B | Normal epithelial cells<br>Basal cell hyperplasia<br>Mildly atypical squamous metaplasia<br>Columnar cell hyperplasia | No abnormality at present<br>Annual examination |
| C | Moderately atypical squamous metaplasia<br>Hyperplasia of columnar cells with enlarged or deeply stained nuclei | Examination in less than 6 months; follow-up |
| D | Severely atypical squamous metaplasia or some suspicion of malignancy | Immediate detailed work-up |
| E | Malignant cells | Immediate detailed work-up |

*Notes:* Classification is made on the basis of the entire specimen, not on the basis of a single cell.
　　　Classification is made on the basis of the highest grade of atypia, but in cases in which only a few cells are obtained the subject is asked to undergo another examination.
　　　Classification of the degree of squamous metaplastic atypia is made with reference to photographs.

**30–33** Endoscopic findings of central early stage lung cancers: polypoid tumor (**30**); nodular invasion (**31**); superficial invasion (**32**); thickening of a bifurcation (**33**).

atypia from severely atypical squamous metaplasia. To make this distinction, the following characteristics are important:

- Large nucleus and enlarged nucleocytoplasmic ratio.
- Increased and nonhomogeneous chromatin.
- Irregular nuclei.
- Strongly stained, thickened cytoplasm.

A distinction between squamous cell carcinoma and severely atypical metaplasia can be made based on a combination of the above parameters, but it is necessary to examine the entire specimen, not just a single cell.

## Criteria for sputum cytology and the significance of the results

The standards for sputum cytology in mass surveys were developed to provide the patient with an easily understandable explanation and to establish a logical and reasonable system in the case of non-definitive results (**Table 4**). With this in mind, it must be remembered that it can be extremely difficult to distinguish between malignant cells with a relatively low degree of atypia and atypical metaplastic cells seen in some non-malignant conditions. Therefore, so as not to overlook an early stage case, any cases of atypical cells must be aggressively followed up until a definitive diagnosis can be reached. In **Table 5** the criteria and responses are based on the degree of atypia, and it can be seen that there is a tendency to place much weight on the evaluation of the degree of atypia of squamous metaplasia. In all conditions that produce atypical metaplastic cells, the authors not only recommend follow-up sputum cytology but also follow-up endoscopy. It is most important to be able to correctly determine whether the cells are from a carcinoma lesion, whether they are suspicious of malignancy, or whether they are from a benign lesion. That is why such criteria for screening for early stage lung cancer, taking the different types of growth into account, are necessary.

### High-risk groups

While sputum cytology is necessary for the detection of central early stage lung cancer, this approach is most effective in high-risk groups.

Almost all central early stage lung cancers are squamous cell carcinomas and the overwhelming majority occur in elderly male heavy smokers, which means that sputum cytology in such a population would be most effective.

Subjects for mass surveys include individuals over 40 years old who undergo chest radiography and sputum cytology is indicated if the patient is:

- Aged 50 or over, with a cigarette index of 600 or over, or
- aged 40 or over, with an episode of bloody sputum within the past 6 months, or
- engaged in an occupation linked to carcinogenesis.

In daily clinical practice, the above three criteria can be employed to determine whether to recommend sputum cytology. As mentioned in the section on symptoms, even if the patient has not experienced bloody sputum, a productive cough over a long period is one symptom for which sputum cytology should be recommended. In Japan, the cost of the examination is approximately ¥2,200 (US$17) and is covered by the Elderly Health Act.

### ENDOSCOPY

If cancer cells are detected in sputum cytology but no abnormal shadow is seen on chest radiography, fiberoptic bronchoscopy must be employed to localize the lesion. Early stage cancer is often found through sputum cytology and endoscopy examinations performed for other chest conditions; furthermore, multiple primary cancer is not rare. Therefore, careful observation throughout the visual range is required in endoscopy.

For a precise diagnosis of the lesion, cytologic examination by brushing or washing of each bronchus and bifurcation or histologic examination of biopsy tissue using fiberoptic bronchoscopy is necessary.

### Endoscopic findings

According to the revised classification of bronchoscopic findings of the Committee on Classification of Bronchoscopic Findings of the Japan Lung Cancer Society, endoscopic findings are classified as primarily mucosal or primarily sub-mucosal. Early stage cancer is a mucosal pathological change exhibiting a primarily mucosal appearance that reflects the type of development.

Polypoid tumors, attached to the bronchial wall only at the base, protrude toward the bronchial lumen and a typical lesion moves on respiration (**30**). Nodular protrusions extend into the lumen from a bronchial wall with a mound-like shape and cause stenosis of the lumen (**31**). The surfaces of polypoid tumors and nodular protrusions show granularity, sometimes adhesion of necrotic material, engorgement of capillary vessels, and bleeding. In the superficial invasion lesion, the mucosal surface shows rough granularity, loss of luster, pallor, loss or disruption of mucosal folds, redness, and bleeding; stenosis of the lumen is slight and necrotic material may adhere to the surface (**32**). If intraepithelial carcinoma occurs at a bronchial bifurcation, the main finding is thickening of the bifurcation (**33**), sometimes accompanied by redness, and endoscopic confirmation may be difficult. If the intraepithelial carcinoma occurs in areas other than a bifurcation, swelling is the main finding; it may be difficult, however, to detect any abnormal findings.

The definition of early stage cancer[2] requires confirmation with a resected specimen (*see* Chapter 1). Therefore, cases that were not resected do not fall into this category. However, there are some cases diagnosed endoscopically and clinically as early stage cancer in which resection cannot be carried out because of poor lung function or complications and which are treated by non-surgical therapeutic methods. Since these cancers must be diagnosed by endoscopy, a proposal for endoscopic criteria for early cancer for non-resectable cases was introduced (**Table 6**).

**Table 5.** Criteria for squamous cell metaplasia in sputum cytology.[8] (This classification can also be used for mass surveys; **bold** type indicates important cytological features.)

| Classification | Appearance | Cytoplasm staining | | Shape of cells | Variability in size | Nucleocyto-plasmic ratio | Shape of the nucleus | Variability in nuclear size | Nuclear border | Chromatin pattern | | | Nucleoli | Multinucleated cells |
|---|---|---|---|---|---|---|---|---|---|---|---|---|---|---|
| | | Light green | Eosin orange | | | | | | | Volume | Pattern | Distribution | | |
| Mildly atypical squamous metaplasia (B) | Cobble stone; flat; cell clusters–loose clusters | **Light staining; uniform** | Light staining; uniform | Polygonal oval | Mild | **Low–moderate**[c] | Oval | Mild | Smooth; uniform | **Mild** | **Fine; lack of structure** | **Almost uniform; scattered** | Unclear–small | Rare |
| Moderately atypical squamous metaplasia (C) | Loose clusters–scattered; occasionally in pairs | **Light staining–slight deep stain; uniform–irregular; occasionally multiple** | Light staining–slight deep stain; almost uniform; occasionally multiple | Oval; polygonal; occasionally irregular | Mild–moderate[b] | **Low–moderate**[c] | Oval; occasionally irregular | Mild–moderate | Smooth–irregular almost uniform | **Mild–moderate**[d] | **Fine; middle granular; lack of structure** | **Almost uniform; scattered** | Unclear–moderate | Occasional; similar nuclear size |
| Severely atypical squamous metaplasia (D)[e] | Irregular cell clusters–scattered but often in pairs | **Light staining–deep staining; Mild–irregular; occasionally multiple** | Deep staining;[a] uniform–irregular; occasionally multiple | Oval–irregular | Mild–moderate[b] | **Low–high** | Oval; occasionally irregular | Moderate–severe | Smooth–irregular; non-uniform thickening | **Moderate;**[d] **rare; severe** | **Fine; rough; lack of structure** | **Slightly non-uniform; scattered–slightly dense** | Unclear–moderate | Often irregular nuclear size |

[a]Deep staining includes both highly distinct and very dark staining.
[b]Moderate variability in size means that the diameter of cytoplasm and nucleus can vary by a factor of 2.
[c]Moderate nucleocytoplasmic ratio means one-half light green staining cytoplasm and one-third eosin orange staining cytoplasm.
[d]Moderate chromatin pattern means nuclear staining equivalent to that of neutrophils.
[e]Category D includes some cases of cancer.

**34**

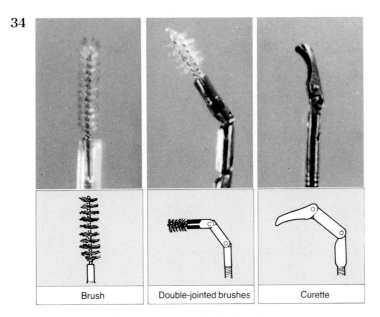

| Brush | Double-jointed brushes | Curette |

**34** Brushes and curettes for cytological brushing.

**35**

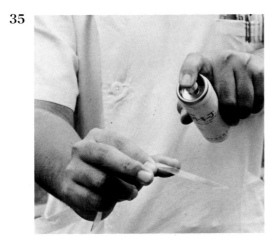

**35** Fixing the cytological specimen with a spray.

**36**

**36** Fixing the cytological specimen by washing the brush. (Matsunami Glass Co., Osaka.)

Although biopsy is required in addition to endoscopic findings (criterion B7) according to this proposal, realistically, there are certain sites at which biopsy cannot be done; furthermore, a biopsy of a large lesion does not necessarily reflect the degree of invasion. In addition, such problems as the difficulty in defining invasion to the outer smooth muscle layer based on biopsy tissue also arise.

In some cases, lymph node metastasis has already taken place by the time carcinoma invasion reaches the outer layer of smooth muscle. Since analysis of endoscopic findings of early cancer without metastasis is as yet insufficient, analysis of more cases is required to fully evaluate early cancer based on endoscopic findings.

To clarify early cancer diagnosis based on endoscopic findings, cases are categorized as thicken-

28

**37**

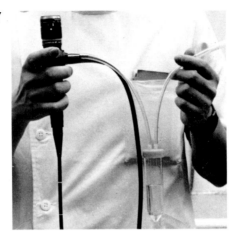

**37** Tube for collecting bronchial lavage cytological specimens (respiratory tract aspiration kit).

ing and swelling, granularity, nodularity, and polyps (*see* Cases — Chapter 3).

## Cytological diagnosis from endoscopic specimens

### Brushing

To diagnose and localize lung cancer lesions accurately, brushing is performed. A brush is inserted through the working channel of the fiberoptic bronchoscope, while the lesion is being observed. Brushing instruments include brushes and curettes (**34**). It is useful to use instruments with a cover to avoid contamination. Not only for protrusions but especially for superficial invasion lesions, brushing at the probable site of resection is important. When endoscopic findings are normal, but carcinoma cells are detected from sputum cytology, it is necessary to brush each bifurcation and peripheral bronchus.

**Table 6.** Proposed criteria for classifying the endoscopic findings of early stage lung cancer[8, 9]

Many hilar (central) early stage squamous cell carcinomas have been detected as a result of improvements in diagnostic techniques. However, since early stage cancer is defined as 'cancer limited to the bronchial wall that has not metastasized and which is confirmed on the resected specimen', nonsurgically treated cases are not included, even if they were probably early stage cancers.

The main diagnostic technique for hilar early stage squamous cell carcinoma is bronchoscopy. Therefore, depending on the case, it must fulfill the criteria for central early stage squamous cell carcinoma, clinically and endoscopically. The following are proposed criteria, primarily based on bronchoscopic findings, for early stage squamous cell carcinoma.

*Category A: Clinical criteria for hilar (central) early stage squamous cell carcinoma:*

1. Chest radiographs (includes tomograms and CT) – normal findings or secondary changes.

2. Clinically, no lymph node or distant metastasis.

*Category B: Endoscopic criteria for hilar (central) early stage squamous cell carcinoma:*

1. Mucosa: paleness, opacity, loss of luster, roughness, microgranularity.
2. Mucosal folds: lack of clarity, thickening, disappearance.
3. Subepithelial blood vessels: disappearance or disruption.
4. Small nodular tumor or swelling in the bronchial lumen.
5. The lesion is located in a site from the main bronchus to subsegmental bronchi.
6. The peripheral area of tumor invasion can be confirmed endoscopically.
7. On biopsy, tumor invasion is limited to the smooth muscle layer.

Criteria B1–4 are restricted to endoscopic findings, and should fulfill the conditions of criteria B5–7.
Cases that fulfil the above criteria can be diagnosed as hilar (central) early stage squamous cell carcinoma.

29

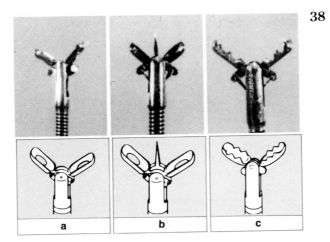

**38** Types of biopsy forceps: (a) forceps with aperture in cups; (b) forceps with needle at the joint; (c) alligator jaw forceps.

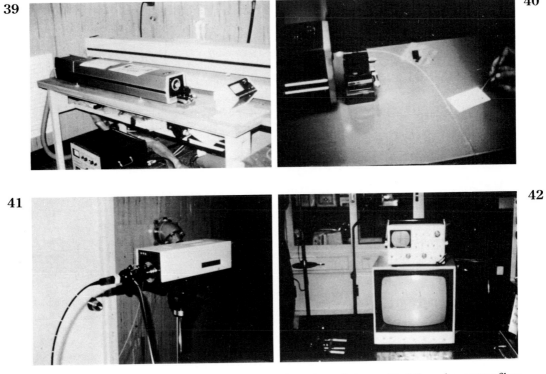

**39–42** TMC system: krypton ion laser (**39**); the laser beam is transmitted through a quartz fiber (**40**); fiberoptic bronchoscope connected to an ultrasensitive television camera (**41**); television monitor (**42**).

**43** 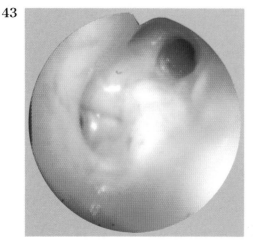 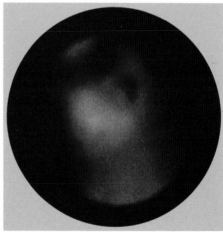 **44**

**43, 44** Strong fluorescence can be seen from this early stage lung cancer (squamous cell carcinoma in the right upper lobe bronchus).

Specimens obtained directly by brushing contain far fewer mucus elements than sputum and dry easily when smear specimens are made. This must be absolutely avoided since a dried specimen can cause misdiagnosis of the cancer cells. The specimen from the brush used in brushing the lesion must be smeared on a glass slide and fixed immediately. When using a curette, the specimen should be expelled by tapping gently against the glass slide. Cell fixation can be done either by immediate immersion in ethanol, by spraying with isopropanol (**35**), or by a brush washing method (**36**).

*Washing cytology*
If identification endoscopically is difficult, because the lesion is extremely small or at a site where it cannot be visualized by endoscopy, washing cytology (**37**) is performed. Usually, the fiberoptic bronchoscope is fixed at the orifice of a lobar or segmental bronchus and approximately 20 ml of saline is injected through the working channel of the fiberoptic bronchoscope. Then, washing fluid is aspirated using a bronchial suction kit and the cell contents concentrated by centrifugation to determine the presence or absence of cancer cells. Suction must be performed thoroughly and carefully so that the washing fluid does not enter the other bronchi. Bronchi with minimal abnormal findings should be washed first to minimize the risk of contamination.

It is necessary to label the exact site from which each specimen is obtained when performing multiple brushing or washing procedures. Cells collected directly from a lesion differ from exfoliated cells in sputum, usually consisting of many cancer cells, forming clusters, and having a greater frequency of non-keratotic cancer cells.

**Endoscopic histology**
Specimens are obtained from lesions within the visual range of the bronchus, but biopsy of a lesion on the lateral wall of a large bronchus may be difficult. For biopsy, forceps are inserted through the working channel of a fiberoptic bronchoscope. There are conventional biopsy forceps, biopsy forceps with apertures in the cups, biopsy forceps with a needle, and alligator jaw forceps (**38**). When performing biopsy, the most suitable forceps to obtain as much material as possible must be used. Forceps with apertures in the cups crush the tissue less, while forceps with a needle at the joint are used if it is hard to grasp the lesion. Any necrotic substance on the surface of the lesion should be removed prior to the biopsy.[10] Since the piece of tissue collected is small, it should be fixed in 10% formalin solution after thorough confirmation that it is a tissue specimen and not a clump of mucus, necrosis, or blood. Tissue diagnosis of such small specimens is not easy. Providing all the relevant information on endoscopy, cytology and clinical findings to the pathologist can help in formulating an accurate diagnosis.

Where a lesion cannot be identified clearly, in

**45**

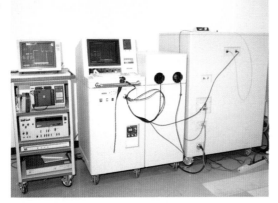

**45** The diagnostic–therapeutic excited dimer laser system.

**46**

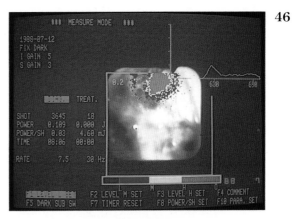

**46** Imaging of the lesion with the excited dimer laser system. Using image processing, the fluorescence from the occult lesion is highlighted and easily recognized.

**47**

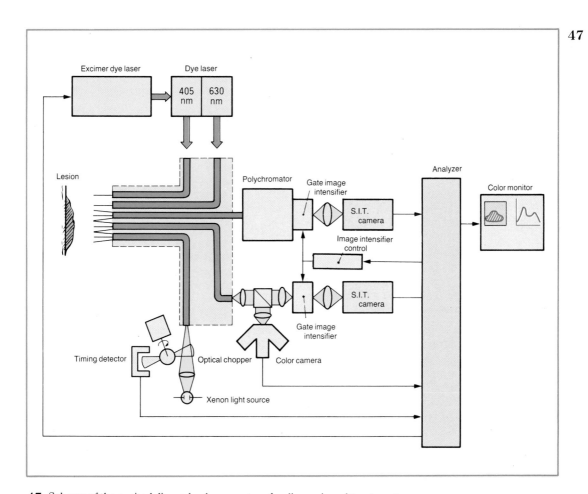

**47** Schema of the excited dimer dye laser system for diagnosis and treatment.

32

49

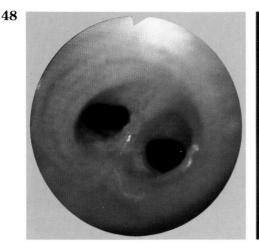 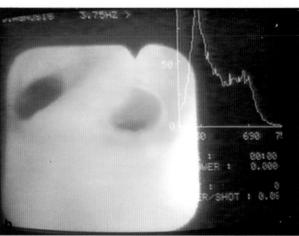

**48, 49** Lesion localization with the excited dimer dye laser system: early stage squamous cell carcinoma at the bifurcation of right $B^3_{ab}$ (**48**); real-time analysis of the wavelength of emitted fluorescence shows strong fluorescence with a pattern typical of HpD *in vivo* (**49**).

spite of the detection of cancer cells in sputum, it must be localized by bronchial washing and brushing as described above. By close observation of the bronchus in which cancer cells were detected, a small lesion of thickening at the bifurcation or swelling can sometimes be found. Biopsy of thickened bifurcations can be pursued aggressively, but determination of the bronchus containing the lesion by cytology is also efficient.

**Photodynamic diagnosis**
Early stage lung cancers detected by sputum cytology that are not indicated on chest radiographs can be so early that the lesion cannot be seen endoscopically. The diagnosis and localization of early cancer lesions is extremely important.

For occult lesions within the endoscopically visible range, photodynamic diagnosis (PDD),[11] a system involving a tumoriphilic photosensitizing agent and laser beams, is being employed.

*Tokyo Medical College (TMC) system*
Hematoporphyrin derivative (HpD) is a tumoriphilic photosensitizing agent absorbed at least 10 times more by tumor tissue than by normal tissue. In normal tissue it is released rapidly, but HpD remains more than 72h in tumor tissue. HpD is strongly excited by ultraviolet radiation of approximately 405 nm wavelength, and releases fluorescent red light at peaks of 630 and 690 nm. Tumor diagnosis, which is peformed by laser

irradiation, makes use of this phenomenon. At a period of 48–72h following intravenous injection of 2.5–5.0 mg/kg of HpD, a 405-nm laser beam, emitted from a krypton ion laser, is transmitted by a 400μ crystal fiber through the biopsy channel of an endoscope, and the fluorescence (630 and 690 nm) from the HpD accumulated in the tumor is observed. Since the fluorescence is too feeble to evaluate macroscopically, the amplified fluorescence is transmitted to a television monitor using an ultrasensitive television camera with a barrier filter of over 610 nm (**39–44, Table 7**).

*Excited dimer system*
Proposed by Aizawa and Kato, an experimental system has been manufactured by Hamamatsu Photonics (Hamamatsu, Shizuoka) and Fuji Film Inc. (Tokyo) with a grant from the Section for Development of Medical Services and Welfare of the Industrial Science and Technology Agency of the Ministry of International Trade and Industry.

The excited dimer laser system (**45**)[12,13] excites XeCl gas (Xe 1.0%, HCl 0.1%) and emits a 308-nm pulse laser beam. DPS ($3.6 \times 10^{-3}$ mol/liter dioxan) with the highest conversion factor when used with a dye laser, is used for diagnosis in order to obtain a 405-nm laser beam to fit the Soret band of HpD. Since the laser is a pulse laser, endoscopy with conventional white light (Xe) is performed during the intervals of nonemission of the laser beam, and the fluorescence from the laser beam irradiation is transmitted to a wavelength analyzer. Since the light path to the

**Table 7.** Results of diagnosis using the krypton ion laser and HpD

| Lung cancer stage | Number of cases | Fluorescence | |
| --- | --- | --- | --- |
| | | Positive | Negative |
| Early stage | 13 | 13 | 0 |
| Advanced stage | 65 | 60 | 5 |
| Total | 78 | 73 | 5 |
| Squamous metaplasia | | | |
| Severe atypia | 5 | 4 | 1 |
| Mild atypia | 1 | 0 | 1 |
| Total | 6 | 4 | 2 |

wavelength analyzer is interrupted upon illumination by white light, endoscopy can be performed simultaneously (**45–47**). Compared with previous systems, endoscopic observation of the lesion can be performed under bright illumination and fluorescence observation is simplified. The fluorescence wavelength is analyzed, amplified with an image intensifier, and finally displayed on the television monitor, together with the endoscopic image (**48, 49**).

HpD has a high affinity for tumors but it is also partially absorbed by inflamed tissue, granulation tissue, and atypical metaplasia. Therefore, HpD fluorescence does not necessarily mean tumor, but an abnormality, and definitive diagnosis must depend upon such methods as histology and cytology. However, if a new agent that possesses a higher tumor-specific affinity is developed in the future, it will be possible to make a diagnosis of tumor based on fluorescence more simply.

## REFERENCES

[1]Shimosato, Y. and Amemiya, R. (1976), Growth patterns of hilar type early squamous cell lung cancer, *Clinical Radiology*, **21**, 987–998.

[2]Ikeda, S. (1976), *Atlas of Hilar Type Early Lung Cancer*, Igaku-Shoin, Tokyo, pp. 7–13.

[3]Horai, T. and Ueki, A. (1978), The cell concentration method using acetylcysteine for sputum cytology, *Acta Cytol.*, **22**, 580–583.

[4]Saccomano, G. *et al.* (1963), Concentration of carcinoma or atypical cells in sputum, *Acta Cytol.*, **7**, 305–310.

[5]Kato, H. (1987), Appearance of lung cancer cells. The efficacy of sputum cytology for early detection of lung cancer, *Modern Medicine*, **16**, 58–67.

[6]Yahada, K., Horai, T. *et al.* (1987), Cell collection method using dithiothreitol for sputum cytology, *J. Jpn. Soc. Clin. Cytol.*, **26**, 398–403.

[7]Hattori, S. *et al.* (1973), Report of the Committee on the Division of Cytological Criteria for Lung Cancer Diagnosis, *Lung Cancer*, **23**, 653–657.

[8]The Japan Lung Cancer Society (1987), *General Rule for Clinical and Pathological Record of Lung Cancer*, Kanehara, Tokyo.

[9]The Japan Lung Cancer Society (1986), Proposed new classification of bronchoscopic findings in lung cancer, *Lung Cancer*, **26**(1), 1–10.

[10]Oho, K. and Amemiya, R. (1985), *Practical Fiberoptic Bronchoscopy*, Igaku-Shoin, Tokyo.

[11]Kato, H. (1985), Early detection of lung cancer by means of hematoporphyrin derivative fluorescence and laser photoradiation, *Clinics in Chest Medicine*, **6**, 237–253.

[12]Kato, H., Aizawa, K. *et al.* (1986), A diagnostic imaging system for cancer localization using excimer dye laser, *Jpn. J. Cancer Chemother.*, **13**, 1647–1652.

[13]Aizawa, K., Ohata, S. *et al.* (1986), Detection of fluorescence spectra of hematoporphyrin derivative in the bronchial tree of beagles using an excimer dye laser, *J. Jpn. Soc. Laser Med.*, **6**, 103–106.

# 3 Cases

## SUMMARY OF ENDOSCOPIC FINDINGS

### Case classification
The endoscopic findings of early stage lung cancer are classified into six categories:

- Thickening and swelling
- Granularity
- Thickening and swelling + granularity
- Nodularity
- Thickening and swelling + nodularity
- Polyps.

Thickening and swelling refers to widened bifurcations and mucosal swelling; nodularity refers to broad-based protruding lesions; granularity refers to ultra-small nodules; and polyps describes pedunculated lesions.

### Endoscopic findings
Related findings of 60 representative cases are summarized in **Table 8** and are discussed below. They included:

- Redness
- Paleness
- Loss of luster
- Vascular engorgement
- Disruption of mucosal folds
- Lack of clarity of mucosal folds
- Irregularity
- Edematous change (small vesicles)
- Necrotic material
- Bleeding.

Lesions with thickening and swelling accounted for 19 cases (30%). The most common related findings were mucosal irregularity (68%) and lack of clarity of mucosal folds (58%). Granular lesions accounted for 6 cases (9%): the most

**Table 8.** Classification of endoscopic findings of early stage lung cancer cases

| Accompanying finding | Findings (lesions) | | | | | |
|---|---|---|---|---|---|---|
| | Thickening and swelling (19) | Granularity (6) | Nodularity (18) | Polyps (7) | Thickening and swelling + granularity (4) | Thickening and swelling + nodularity (10) |
| Redness | 10 (53%) | 2 (33%) | 7 (39%) | 2 (29%) | 1 (25%) | 4 (40%) |
| Paleness | 1 (5%) | 2 (33%) | 5 (28%) | | 1 (25%) | 1 (10%) |
| Lack of luster | 7 (37%) | 2 (33%) | 6 (33%) | 2 (29%) | 3 (75%) | 2 (20%) |
| Vascular engorgement | 1 (5%) | | 1 (6%) | | | |
| Disruption of mucosal folds | | 1 (17%) | 2 (11%) | | | 1 (10%) |
| Loss of clarity of mucosal folds | 11 (58%) | 2 (33%) | 5 (28%) | | 3 (75%) | 10 (100%) |
| Mucosal irregularity | 13 (68%) | 4 (67%) | 13 (72%) | 1 (14%) | 3 (75%) | 10 (100%) |
| Edematous change (small vesicles) | 2 (11%) | | 7 (39%) | 4 (57%) | | 4 (40%) |
| Necrotic material | | 3 (50)% | 3 (17%) | 3 (43%) | | 4 (40%) |
| Bleeding | | | | 1 (14%) | 1 (25%) | 4 (40%) |

common related findings were mucosal irregularity (67%), followed by moss-like adhesion (necrotic material) (50%).

Lesions with thickening and swelling + granularity only accounted for 4 cases (6%): they were accompanied by irregularity of mucosal folds (75%) and lack of clarity of mucosal folds (75%). In the 18 cases (28%) of nodular lesions, mucosal irregularity was seen in 72%, followed by edematous (small vesicles) change (39%), redness (39%), and lack of clarity of mucosal folds (28%).

Lesions with thickening and swelling + nodularity represented only 10 cases (16%): in all of these loss of clarity of mucosal folds and mucosal irregularity were observed and edema (small vesicles) were seen in 40% of the cases.

There were polyps in 6 cases (10%): edematous findings were seen in 57% and moss-like adhesion (necrotic material) was seen in 43% of the cases.

## ENDOSCOPIC APPEARANCE OF THE NORMAL BRONCHUS

The tracheobronchial tree is shown in **50**, and the endoscopic images of the normal bronchus are shown in **51–66**.

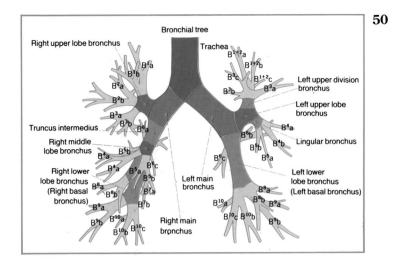

**50** Bifurcations of the tracheobronchial tree. (From Hayata, Y. and Kato, H., Collection of endoscopic slides on early stage lung cancer; Maruzen, 1988.)

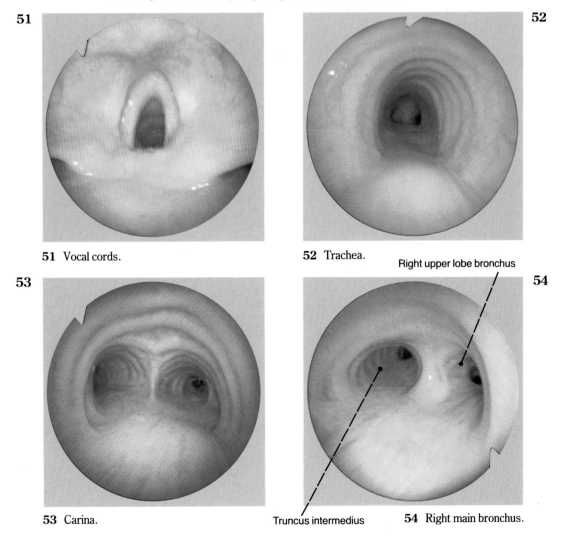

**51** Vocal cords.

**52** Trachea.

**53** Carina.

Truncus intermedius

**54** Right main bronchus.

Right upper lobe bronchus

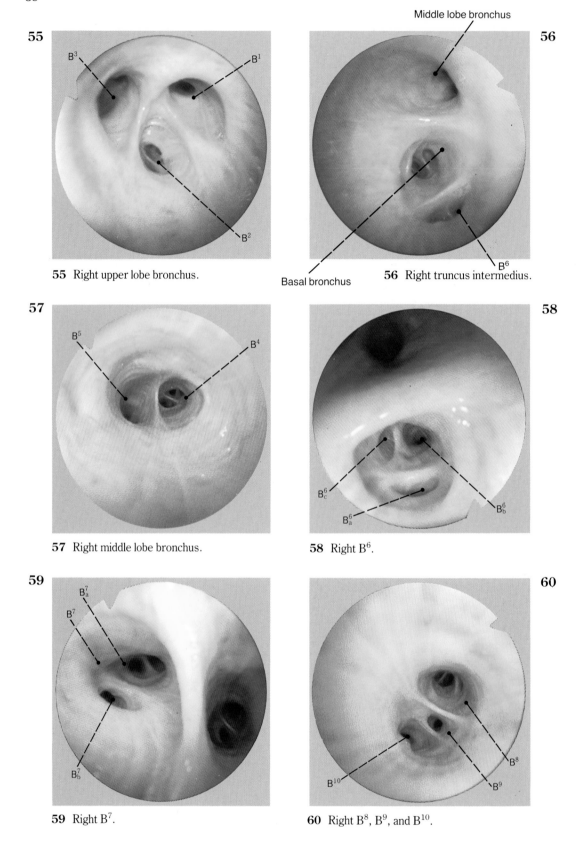

**55** Right upper lobe bronchus.

**56** Right truncus intermedius.

**57** Right middle lobe bronchus.

**58** Right B$^6$.

**59** Right B$^7$.

**60** Right B$^8$, B$^9$, and B$^{10}$.

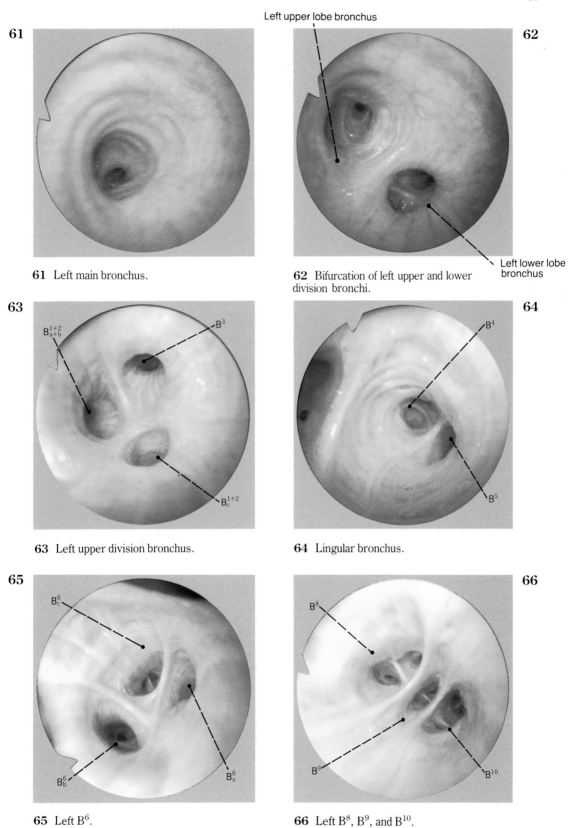

**61** Left main bronchus.

**62** Bifurcation of left upper and lower division bronchi.

**63** Left upper division bronchus.

**64** Lingular bronchus.

**65** Left $B^6$.

**66** Left $B^8$, $B^9$, and $B^{10}$.

# Cases

Thickening and swelling     16 cases

Granularity     5 cases

Thickening and swelling + granularity     4 cases

Nodularity     14 cases

Thickening and swelling + nodularity     10 cases

Polyps     6 cases

Multiple incidence     4 cases

## THICKENING AND SWELLING — 1

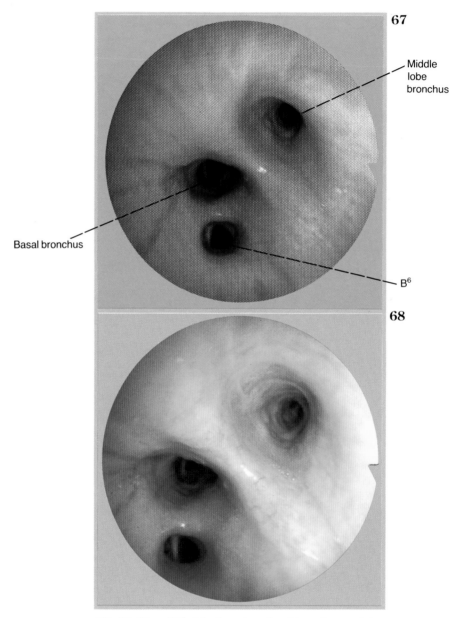

**67**

Middle
lobe
bronchus

Basal bronchus

B$^6$

**68**

**67, 68** The middle lobe bronchus, basal bronchus, and the orifice of B$^6$ are slightly swollen and thickened.

*Patient:* 72-year-old male, unemployed.
*Smoking history:* 20/day, about 50 years.
*Family history:* Nothing in particular.
*Past history:* Nothing in particular.
*Reason for detection:* Atypical cells were detected by sputum cytology. Chest radiograph was normal. Bronchoscopy revealed redness, swelling, and thickening at the orifice of right middle and lower lobe bronchus and B⁶. A diagnosis of squamous cell carcinoma was made by brushing and biopsy of the orifice of B⁶ and the middle lobe. (*Tokyo Medical College Hospital*)

**69**

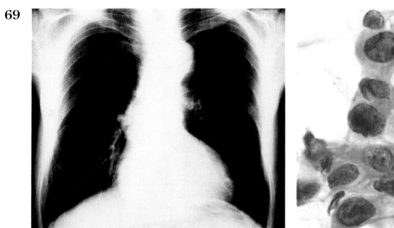

**69** Chest radiograph does not reveal any abnormalities.

**70**

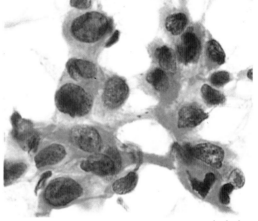

**70** Brushing specimen reveals squamous cell carcinoma with little nuclear atypia (×*400*).

**71**

Basal bronchus      Middle lobe bronchus

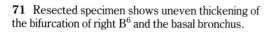

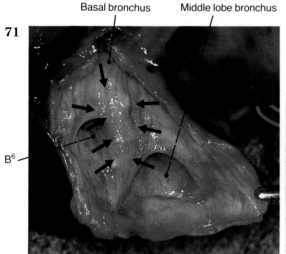

B⁶

**71** Resected specimen shows uneven thickening of the bifurcation of right B⁶ and the basal bronchus.

**72**

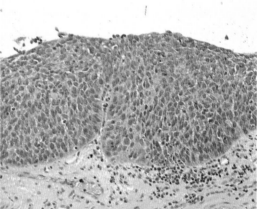

**72** Histological findings of the resected specimen show an *in situ* carcinoma that consists of small cells. No submucosal invasion is detected (×*100*).

## THICKENING AND SWELLING — 2

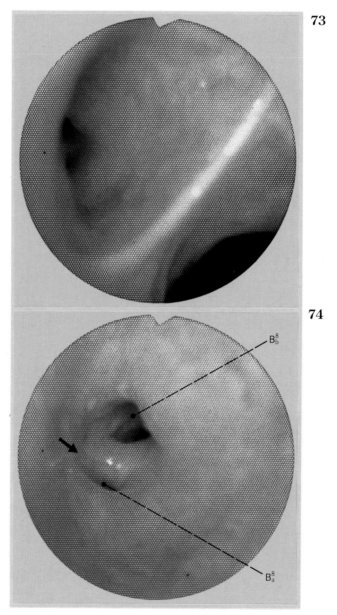

**73**

**74**

**73, 74** No abnormalities detected other than slight redness at the orifice of left $B^8$ (**73**). Mucosa of the bifurcation of left $B_a^8$ and $B_b^8$ is edematous and the normal luster is lost (**74**).

*Patient:* 65-year-old male, bookshop owner.
*Smoking history:* 40/day, 38 years.
*Family history:* Nothing in particular.
*Past history:* Pulmonary tuberculosis (age 26), diabetes (age 50).
*Reason for detection:* Although asymptomatic, mass survey sputum cytology revealed squamous cell carcinoma. (*Center for Adult Diseases, Osaka*)

**75**　　　　**76**　　　　**77**

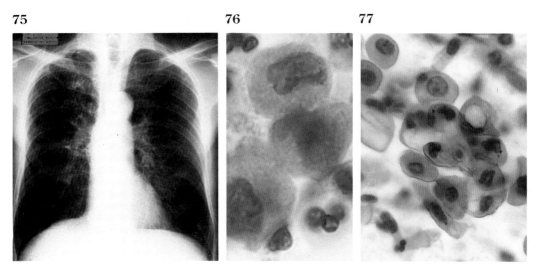

**75** Chest radiograph only shows old pulmonary TB.

**76** Mass survey sputum cytology (×*1000*).

**77** Bronchial washing cytology (× *400*).

**78**　　　　**79**

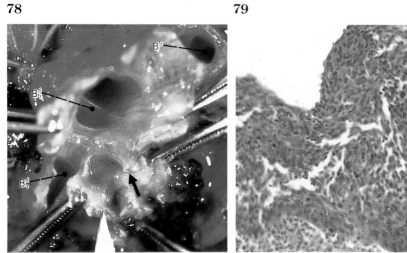

**78** At resection, the mucosa of left B⁸ has microgranularity.

**79** Histological findings of the resected specimen show partial infiltration along the duct and moderately differentiated squamous cell carcinoma almost completely limited to the epithelium (×*100*).

## THICKENING AND SWELLING — 3

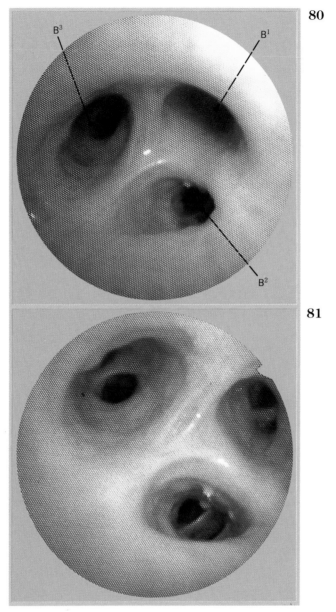

**80, 81** Slight thickening was detected in $B^1$ and $B^2$ in the trifurcating upper lobe bronchus. The mucosal folds have disappeared and small granules are seen in right $B^2$.

*Patient:* 66-year-old male, unemployed.
*Smoking history:* 20/day, 48 years since age 18.
*Family history:* Nothing in particular.
*Past history:* Pulmonary tuberculosis about 15 years previously, treated for several years.
*Reason for detection:* Bloody sputum appeared about 2 months previously and sputum cytology revealed squamous cell carcinoma. He had occasional bloody sputum for 15 years. (*Kinki Central Hospital*)

**82**

**83**          **84**

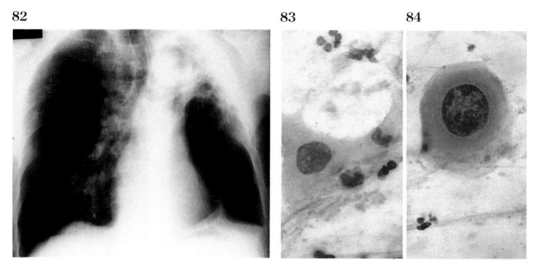

**82** Chest radiograph shows sclerotic tuberculosis in the left upper lobe with cavity (the cause of bloody sputum).

**83, 84** Sputum cytology shows squamous cell carcinoma (×400).

**85**

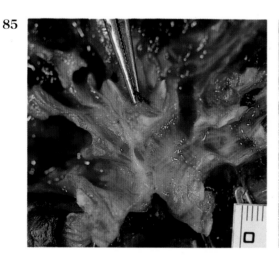

**86**

**85** The resected specimen. Mucosal thickening and loss of mucosal folds are seen at the bifurcation of right B$^1$ and B$^2$. The tumor occupies the bifurcation.

**86** Low-power magnification of the orifice of right B$^2$ shows squamous cell carcinoma, mostly consisting of intraepithelial carcinoma with partial microinvasion.

**THICKENING AND SWELLING — 4**

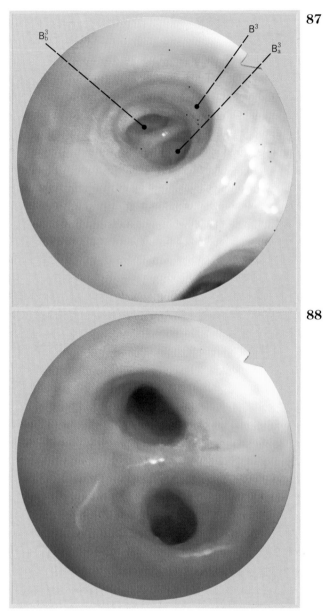

**87, 88** The bifurcation of right $B_a^3$ and $B_b^3$ shows slight thickening.

*Patient:* 58-year-old male, company employee.
*Smoking history:* 20–30/day, about 40 years.
*Family history:* Elder brother died of lung cancer.
*Past history:* Left pulmonary tuberculosis (age 27); operated on for spondylolysis (age 33); oscheohydrocele (traumatic, age 38); operated on for gastric ulcer (age 46).
*Reason for detection:* Squamous cell carcinoma detected by sputum cytology at lung cancer mass survey. No abnormal shadows, apart from pulmonary fibrosis, were recognized from the chest radiograph. (*Tokyo Medical College Hospital*)

**89**

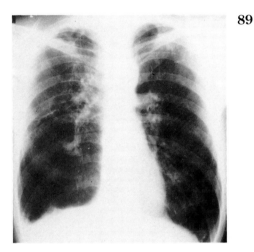

**89** Chest radiograph shows no tumor shadow.

**90**

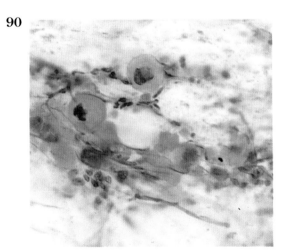

**91**

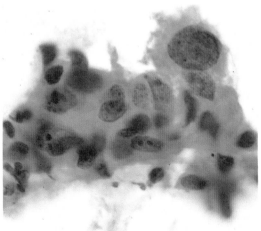

**90** Small keratinized squamous cell carcinoma cells detected in sputum cytology (×*400*).

**91** A group of unevenly sized squamous carcinoma cells with increased chromatin (×*400*).

## THICKENING AND SWELLING — 5

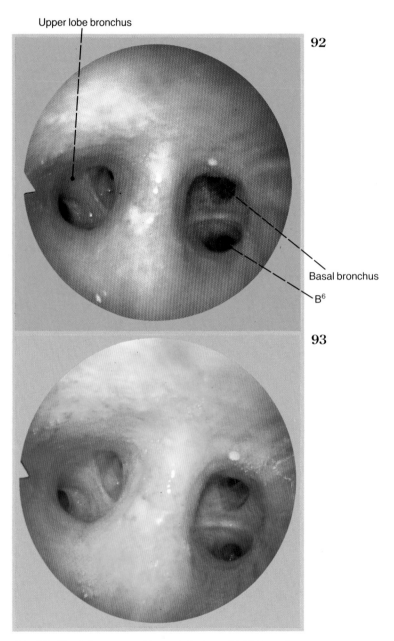

**92, 93** The left upper and lower lobe bronchial bifurcation is thickened. A slight mucosal irregularity in the upper anterior wall is detected.

*Patient:* 68-year-old male, unemployed.
*Smoking history:* 20/day, 50 years.
*Family history:* Nothing in particular.
*Past history:* Nothing in particular.
*Reason for detection:* Cough and sputum for 6 months previously. Chest radiograph mass survey was negative, but he was referred to a hospital after sputum cytology diagnosed positive. (*Tokyo Medical College Hospital*)

**94**

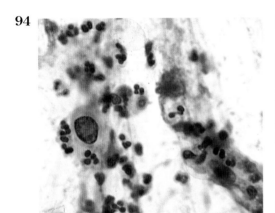

**95**

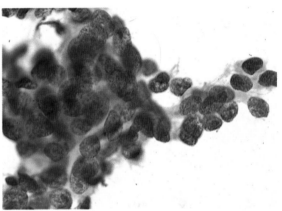

**94** A group of non-keratinized squamous carcinoma cells detected in sputum cytology.

**95** A group of non-keratinized squamous carcinoma cells obtained by brushing cytology.

**96**

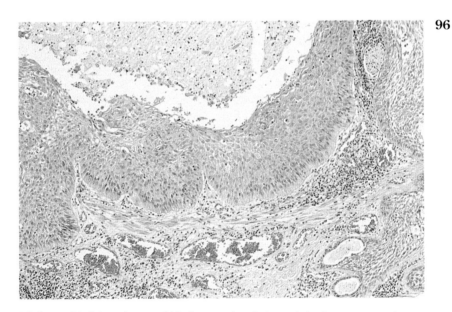

**96** Intraepithelial carcinoma which does not invade beyond the basement membrane (×*40*).

## THICKENING AND SWELLING — 6

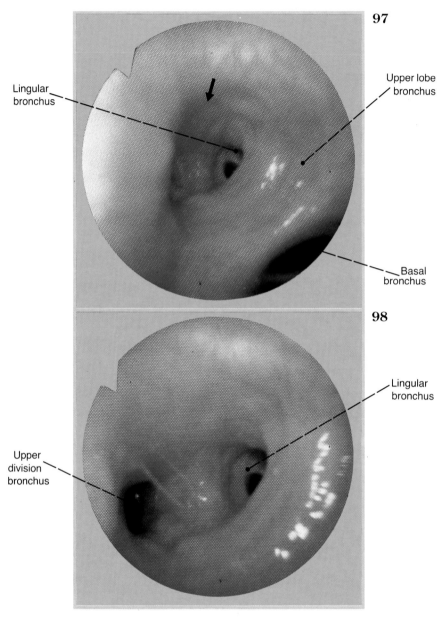

**97**

Lingular bronchus

Upper lobe bronchus

Basal bronchus

**98**

Lingular bronchus

Upper division bronchus

**97, 98** Redness and unevenness was detected in the mucosa of the left upper lobe bronchus, and swelling and irregularity of the bifurcation of the lingular and upper division bronchi can be clearly seen.

*Patient:* 47-year-old male, company employee.
*Smoking history:* 30/day, 29 years.
*Family history:* Nothing in particular.
*Past history:* Appendicitis (age 22).
*Reason for detection:* Bloody sputum appeared 1 month before detailed examination for an abnormal shadow detected in a mass survey for gastric cancer. Chest radiograph was negative, but squamous cell carcinoma was detected by sputum cytology. (*Center for Adult Diseases, Osaka*)

**99**

**99** Brushing cytology (×400).

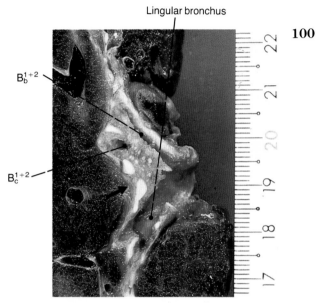

**100**

Lingular bronchus

$B_b^{1+2}$

$B_c^{1+2}$

**100** Posterior aspect of the resected specimen shows a tumor with superficial invasion from the left upper division to the lingular bronchus.

**101**

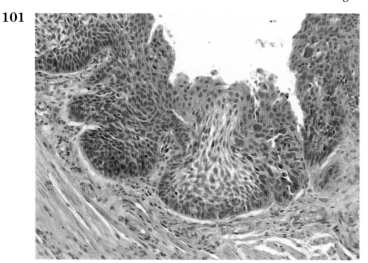

**101** Histological findings show intraepithelial invading squamous cell carcinoma (×100).

## THICKENING AND SWELLING — 7

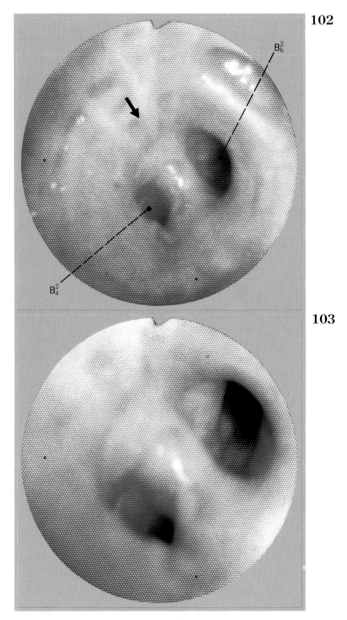

**102, 103** The mucosa of right $B^2$ is edematous with partial irregularity. Thickening of the bifurcation of $B_a^2$ and $B_b^2$ with an uneven surface can be seen.

55

*Patient:* 75-year-old male, unemployed.
*Smoking history:* 20–30/day; 44 years, from age 22 to 68.
*Family history:* Nothing in particular.
*Past history:* Gastric cancer (age 73).
*Reason for detection:* Cough and bloody sputum developed 1 month before he visited a local doctor. Chest radiograph showed pneumonia-like shadows, and sputum cytology revealed squamous cell carcinoma. (*Center for Adult Diseases, Osaka*)

**104**

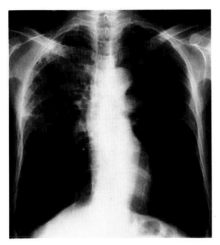

**104** Chest radiograph shows a pneumonia-like shadow in the right upper lobe and tuberculoma in the left upper lobe. No other distinct tumor-like shadow is seen.

**105**

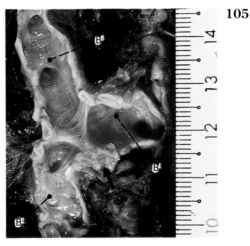

**105** Resected specimen shows irregularity at the orifice of right $B^2$.

**106**

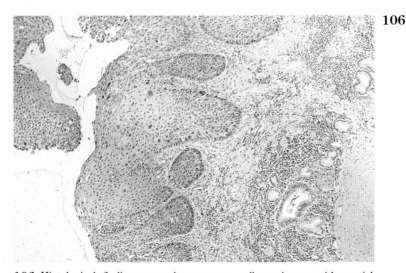

**106** Histological findings reveal squamous cell carcinoma with partial microinvasion in right $B^2$ (×40).

## THICKENING AND SWELLING — 8

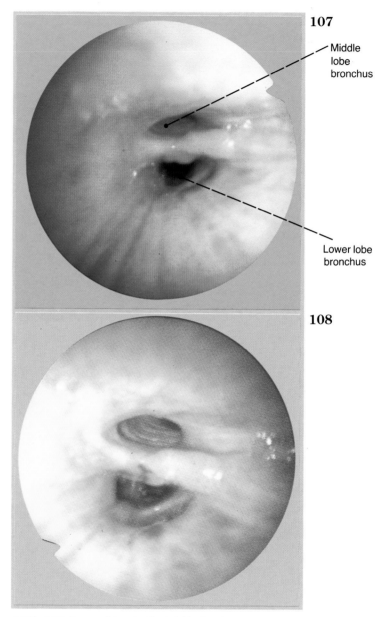

107

Middle
lobe
bronchus

Lower lobe
bronchus

108

**107, 108** Loss of longitudinal folds in the membranous
part of the right truncus intermedius and fine granularity can
be seen (**107**). The bifurcation of the truncus intermedius
and lower lobe bronchus has thickened remarkably, and
granular irregularity can be observed (**108**).

*Patient:* 65-year-old male, foundry worker.
*Smoking history:* 20/day, 45 years.
*Family history:* Nothing in particular.
*Past history:* Gastric ulcer (age 63).
*Reason for detection:* Cough and sputum developed 1 month previously. Chest radiograph was normal, but squamous cell carcinoma was detected by sputum cytology. (*Osaka Habikino Hospital*)

**109**

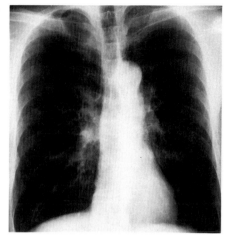

**109** Chest radiograph reveals no abnormality.

Middle lobe bronchus

Lower lobe bronchus

**110**

$B^6$

$B^7$

$B^9 + B^{10}$

$B^8$

**110** Resected specimen shows superficial invasion along the right truncus intermedius, the orifices of the right middle lobe bronchus and lower lobe bronchus, and $B^6$.

**111**

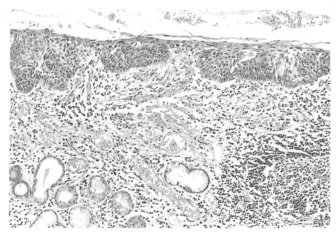

**111** Histological findings of the resected tumor show intraepithelial squamous cell carcinoma ($\times 40$).

## THICKENING AND SWELLING — 9

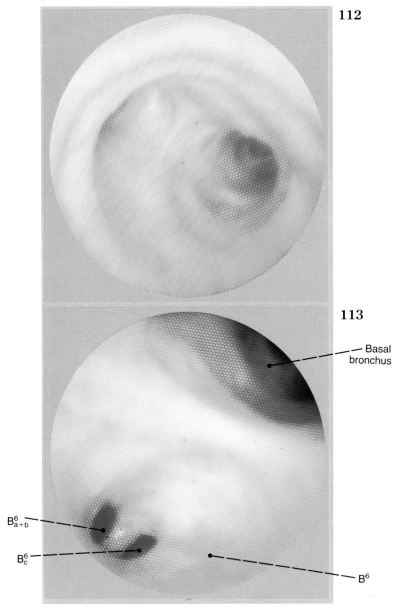

112, 113 Bifurcation of left upper and lower lobe bronchi. The orifice of left $B^6$ can just be seen (112). Thickening of the bifurcation of $B^6_{a+b}$ and $B^6_c$ and loss of mucosal folds can be recognized (113).

*Patient:* 58-year-old male, boilermaker.
*Smoking history:* 60/day, 38 years.
*Family history:* Elder brother died of lung cancer.
*Past history:* Operated on for gastric cancer (age 53).
*Reason for detection:* Sputum cytology in a mass survey revealed squamous cell carcinoma. (*Kinki Central Hospital*)

**114**

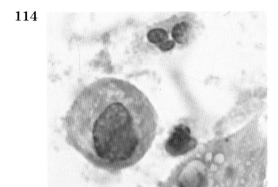

**114** Squamous cell carcinoma detected in sputum cytology specimen (×*1000*).

**115**

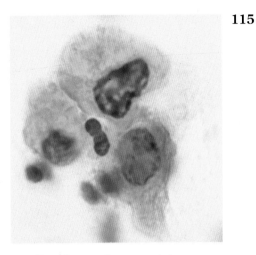

**115** Brushing cytology revealed squamous cell carcinoma in left $B_c^6$ (×*1000*).

**116**

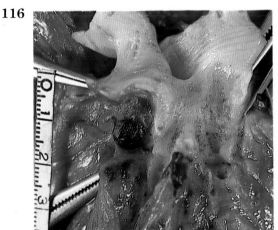

**116** Resected specimen shows mucosal irregularity extending 1 cm from the orifice of left $B_c^6$.

**117**

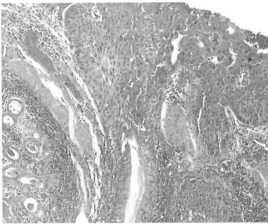

**117** Histological findings of the resected tumor reveal intraepithelial squamous cell carcinoma (×*100*).

# THICKENING AND SWELLING — 10

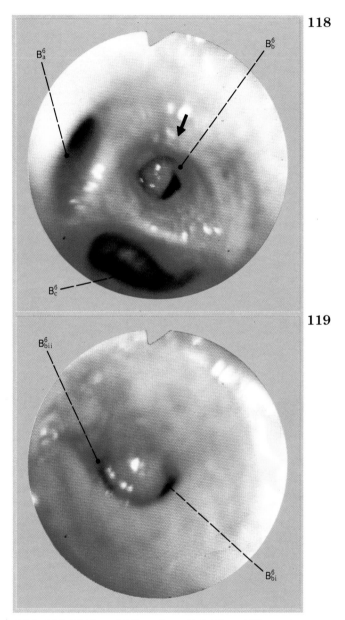

**118, 119** Thickened bifurcation of left $B_{bi}^6$ and $B_{bii}^6$ can be seen.

Patient: 88-year-old male, unemployed.
Smoking history: 30/day, 64 years.
Past history: Gastric ulcer (age 48).
Reason for detection: He had heavy sputum for some time, but had not undergone any specific examinations. Squamous cell carcinoma was detected by sputum cytology. (Center for Adult Diseases, Osaka)

**120**

**121**

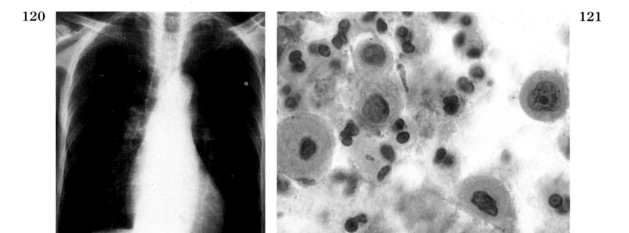

**120** Chest radiograph reveals no abnormality.

**121** Mass survey sputum cytology (×1000).

**122**

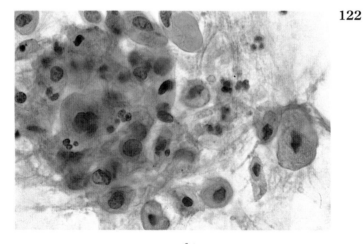

**122** Brushing cytology of the left B⁶ lesion (×400).

## THICKENING AND SWELLING — 11

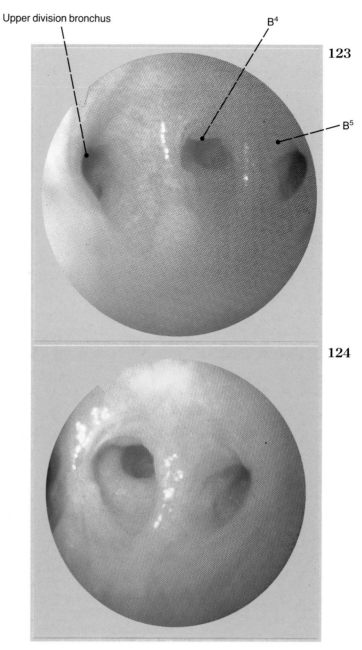

Upper division bronchus

B⁴

B⁵

123

124

**123, 124** The left upper lobe bronchus trifurcates into the upper division, $B^4$, and $B^5$. The bifurcation between the upper division bronchus and $B^4$ is pale and slightly protruding, but histologically, squamous metaplasia was recognized (**123**). Thickening of the bifurcation of $B^4$ and $B^5$, and loss of mucosal folds can be recognized (**124**).

*Patient:* 59-year-old male, company executive.
*Smoking history:* 40/day, 39 years.
*Family history:* Nothing in particular.
*Past history:* Hepatitis (age 57), diabetes (age 59).
*Reason for detection:* He had developed general malaise and palpitations. When hospitalized for detailed examinations, sputum cytology revealed squamous cell carcinoma. (*Kinki Central Hospital*)

**125**

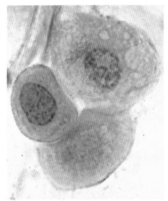

**125** Squamous cell carcinoma detected by sputum cytology (×*1000*).

**126**

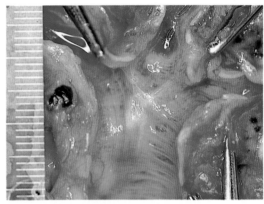

**126** Resected specimen shows thickening of the bifurcation of the upper lobe bronchus and B⁴, but the mucosal folds were confirmed.

**127**

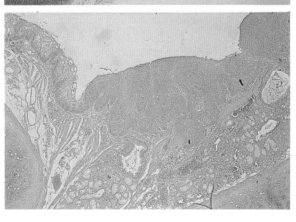

**127** Low-power magnification of the cross-section of the resected left B⁴ and B⁵ shows intraepithelial carcinoma with micro-invasion in part.

**128**

**128** Histological findings of the resected tumor reveal intraepithelial carcinoma with microinvasion (×*40*).

## THICKENING AND SWELLING — 12

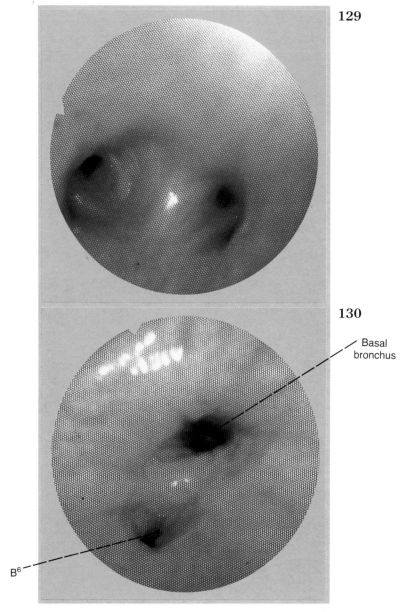

**129, 130** Redness and swelling are detected in wide areas from the bifurcation of the left upper and lower lobe bronchi into both bronchi.

Patient: 81-year-old male.
Smoking history: 15/day, 64 years.
Past history: Nothing in particular.
Reason for detection: Cough and sputum developed 2 months previously, but no abnormality was detected in chest radiograph. Sputum cytology revealed squamous cell carcinoma. (Center for Adult Diseases, Osaka)

**131**

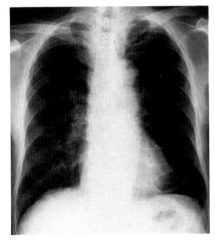

**132**

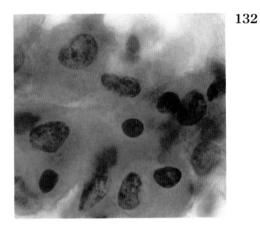

**131** Chest radiograph shows no abnormality.

**132** Sputum cytology (×1000).

**133**

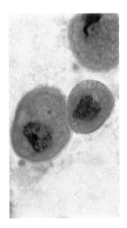

**134**

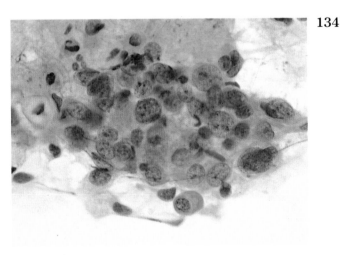

**133** Sputum cytology (×1000).

**134** Brushing cytology (×400).

## THICKENING AND SWELLING — 13

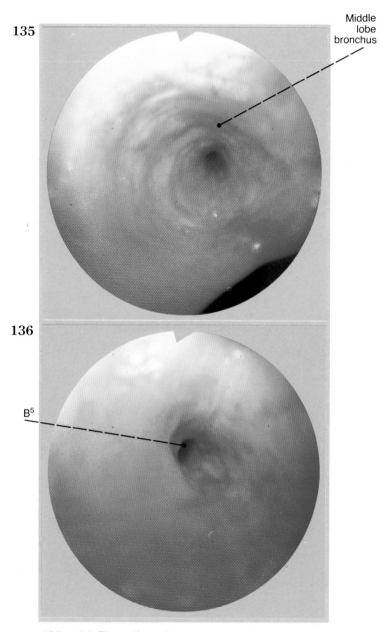

**135** **136** The orifice of the right middle lobe bronchus shows redness, stenosis, and swelling (**135**). In the lower photograph, $B^5$ could be identified but not $B^4$ (**136**).

Patient: 81-year-old male, unemployed.
Smoking history: 20/day, 55 years.
Family history: Nothing in particular.
Past history: Hypertension (age 60).
Reason for detection: Cough and sputum had developed 10 years previously. On a health check-up 1 month previously, there was no abnormal shadow on the chest radiograph, but sputum cytology was positive. Bronchoscopic biopsy and brushing revealed squamous cell carcinoma. (Tokyo Medical College Hospital)

**137**

**138**

**137**, **138** Abnormally shaped cells contain orange G and blue-green stained cytoplasm. Squamous cell carcinoma (×400).

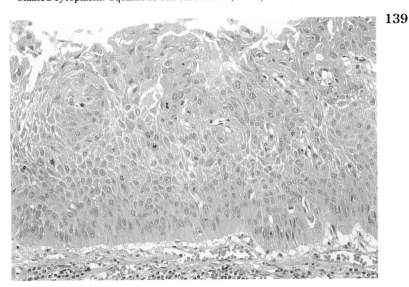

**139**

**139** Histological findings of the resected tumor reveal squamous cell carcinoma and suggest submucosal invasion (×100).

# THICKENING AND SWELLING — 14

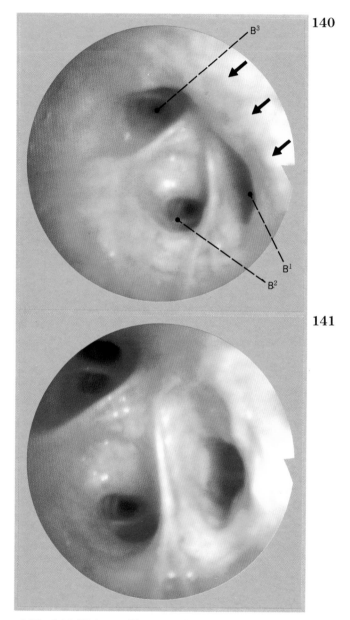

**140, 141** Slight swelling was detected in the anterio-superior wall of the right upper lobe bronchus. The mucosa is irregular from the orifice to the peripheral area of $B^1$. Brushing cytology of this lesion was performed since biopsy in this area is technically difficult.

Patient: 36-year-old male, civil servant.
Smoking history: 30/day, 15 years.
Family history: Nothing in particular.
Past history: Sinusitis (age 15).
Reason for detection: Squamous cell carcinoma was detected by sputum cytology in a mass survey. No abnormality can be recognized on chest radiograph. (Tokyo Medical College Hospital)

**142**

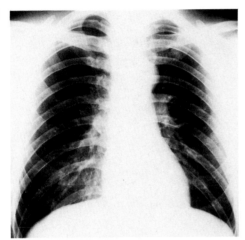

**142** Chest radiograph reveals no abnormality.

**143**

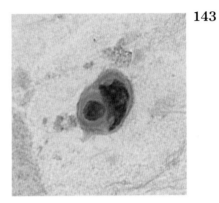

**143** Squamous cell carcinoma with keratinization detected in sputum cytology (×400).

**144**

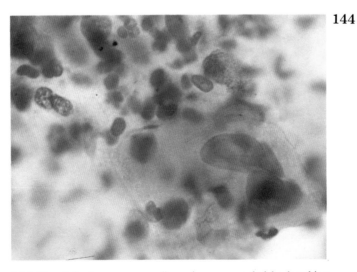

**144** Keratinized squamous cell carcinoma revealed by brushing cytology (×400).

## THICKENING AND SWELLING — 15

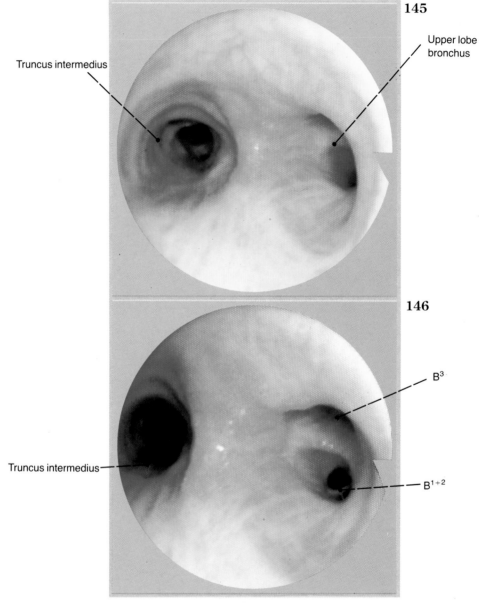

**145**

Upper lobe
bronchus

Truncus intermedius

**146**

B³

Truncus intermedius

B¹⁺²

**145, 146** Redness and swelling of the mucosa was recognized from the orifice of the right upper lobe to the bifurcation of the segmental bronchi.

*Patient:* 69-year-old male, leather industry worker.
*Smoking history:* 15/day, 48 years.
*Family history:* Nothing in particular.
*Past history:* Appendicitis (age 60).
*Reason for detection:* Had a fever of 39°C 1 month before visiting a doctor. Fever disappeared after antibiotic administration, but an abnormal shadow was detected on the chest radiograph. Early stage lung cancer with superficial invasion at the orifice of right upper lobe was detected by bronchoscopic fiberoscopy. The abnormal shadow in the left lung was an advanced lung cancer. (*Center for Adult Diseases, Osaka*)

**147** Brushing cytology at the orifice of the right upper lobe bronchus (×*400*).

**147**

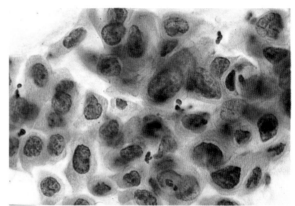

**148** Brushing cytology at the orifice of the right upper lobe bronchus (×*1000*).

**148**

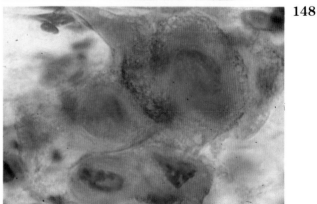

**149** Histological finding of biopsy from the orifice of the right upper lobe (×*100*).

**149**

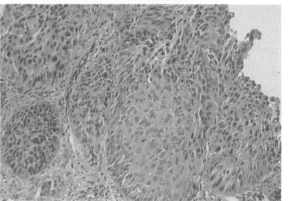

## THICKENING AND SWELLING — 16

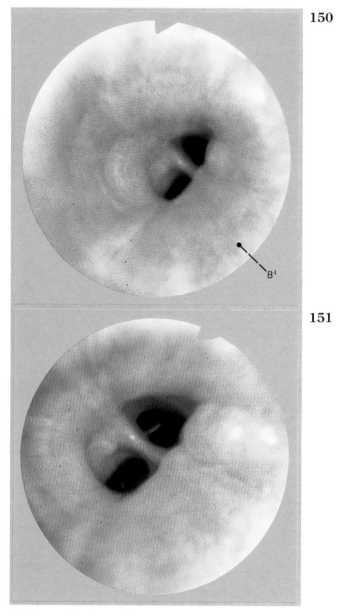

**150**

**151**

**150, 151** In right B⁴ a slight swelling was recognized immediately proximal to the bifurcation of the subsegmental bronchi.

73

> *Patient:* 59-year-old male, *tofu* (soybean curd) manufacturer.
> *Smoking history:* 20/day, 45 years.
> *Family history:* Both parents died of gastric cancer.
> *Past history:* Hypertension (since age 26).
> *Reason for detection:* Occasional cough and sputum for some time prompted participation in mass survey. Sputum cytology revealed squamous carcinoma cells; radiograph was negative. (*Center for Adult Diseases, Osaka*)

**152**

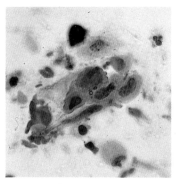

**152** Mass survey cytological specimen treated by the mucolytic method (×*400*).

**153**

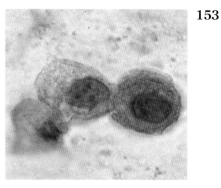

**153** Direct smear method sputum cytology (×*1000*).

**154**

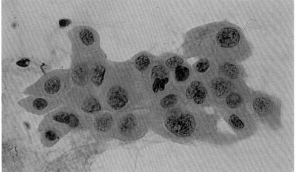

**154** Brushing specimen (×*400*).

**155**

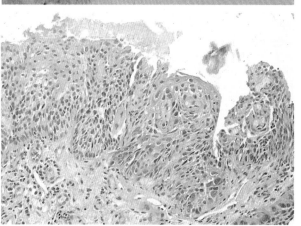

**155** Biopsy specimen reveals squamous cell carcinoma with microscopic invasion (×*100*).

## GRANULARITY – 1

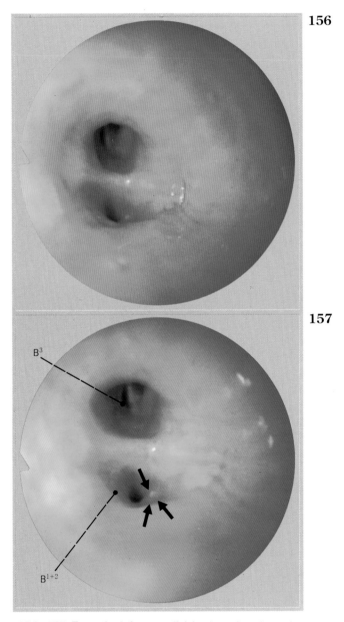

**156, 157** From the left upper division bronchus the endoscopic findings show a small granule (0.5 mm) in left $B^{1+2}$. Mucosal folds appear normal. The white areas at the orifice of $B^{1+2}$ are adherent secretions.

*Patient:* 58-year-old female, unemployed.
*Smoking history:* 40/day, 37 years.
*Family history:* Nothing in particular.
*Past history:* Chronic rheumatoid arthritis since age 57.
*Reason for detection:* Cough had developed 2 months previously, at night and in the morning after smoking. Sputum cytology revealed squamous cell carcinoma. Chest radiograph was normal. (*Tokyo Medical College Hospital*)

**158**

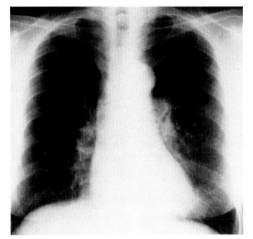

**158** Chest radiograph does not reveal any abnormality.

**159**

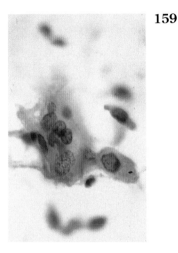

**159** The brushing specimen reveals keratinized squamous carcinoma cells (×400).

**160**

B³  B¹⁺²  Lingular bronchus

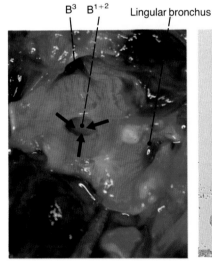

**160** At resection, thickening of the left B¹⁺² orifice was recognized.

**161**

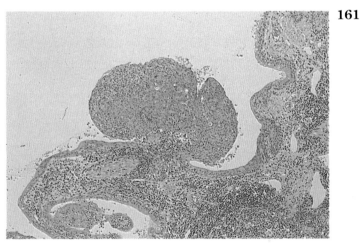

**161** Histological findings of the resected specimen show squamous cell carcinoma but submucosal invasion is unclear. Squamous metaplasia can be seen in the surrounding area (×40).

## GRANULARITY — 2

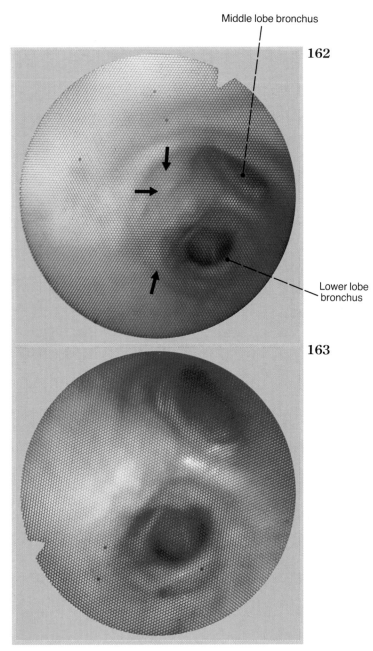

**162, 163** Endoscopic view from the right truncus intermedius shows irregularity and granularity at the bifurcation
of the right middle and lower lobe bronchus.

Patient: 64-year-old male, glue manufacturer.
Smoking history: 15/day, 44 years.
Family history: Nothing in particular.
Past history: High blood pressure (since age 54), gastric polyp (age 61).
Reason for detection: Productive cough developed 1 year previously, but chest radiograph was normal. Sputum cytology yielded a diagnosis of squamous cell carcinoma. (Center for Adult Diseases, Osaka)

**164** Sputum cytology specimen (×400).

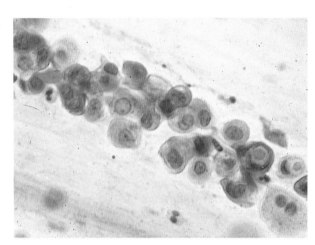

**164**

**165** Resected truncus intermedius, opened from the posterior aspect, shows granular changes at the bifurcation between the right middle lobe bronchus and the lower lobe bronchus.

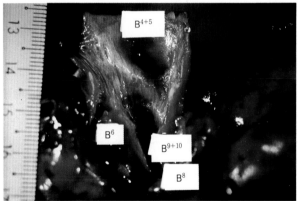

**165**

**166** Histological findings of the resected specimen show that the invasion is limited to within the bronchial mucosa (×40).

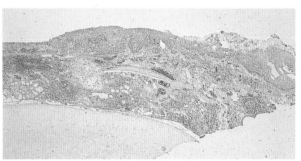

**166**

78

## GRANULARITY — 3

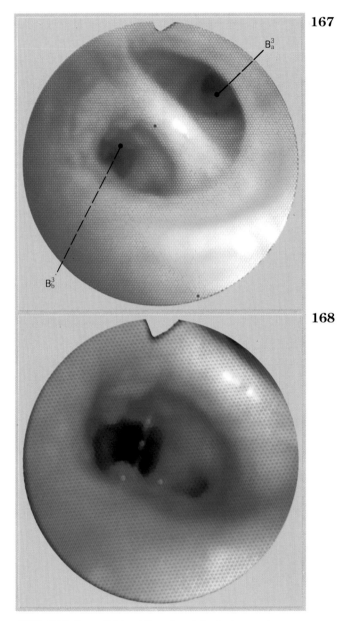

**167**

**168**

**167, 168** A small (about 1 mm) nodular lesion can be seen in $B_b^3$ (**167**). Small nodules can be seen in the anterior and posterior walls of $B_b^3$ (**168**). Findings viewed through a 4-mm diameter fiberoptic bronchoscope.

*Patient:* 64-year-old male, company executive.
*Smoking history:* 30/day, 40 years.
*Family history:* Nothing in particular.
*Past history:* Nothing in particular.
*Reason for detection:* A survey-by-mail sputum cytology examination revealed squamous cell carcinoma. Chest radiograph was normal. (*Tokyo Medical College Hospital*)

**169**

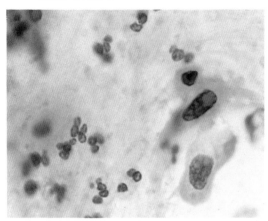

**170**

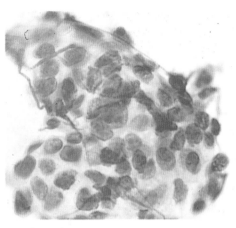

**169** Keratotic squamous cell carcinoma cells in the sputum specimen (×*400*).

**170** Brushing specimen reveals a cluster of cells with non-keratotic cytoplasm (×*400*).

**171**

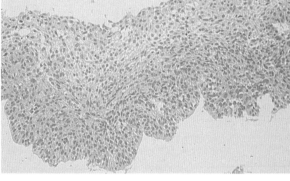

**171** Biopsy reveals squamous cell carcinoma (×*100*).

**172**

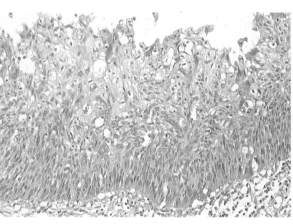

**172** Resected specimen shows well-differentiated squamous cell carcinoma with a distinct tendency to keratinization. The presence of submucosal invasion is uncertain (×*200*).

**GRANULARITY — 4**

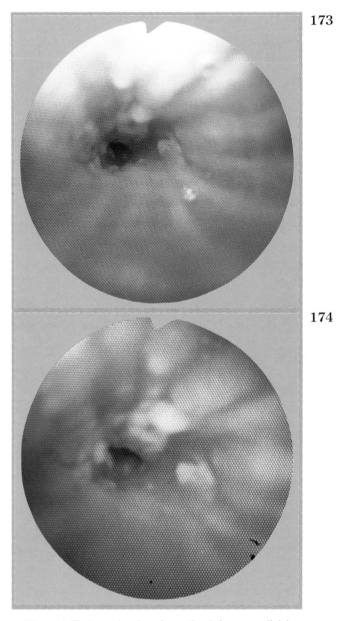

173

174

**173**, **174** Endoscopic view from the left upper division bronchus reveals multiple small granular nodules in $B_{a+b}^{1+2}$ with disruption of longitudinal folds.

Patient: 62-year-old male, farmer.
Smoking history: 10–20/day, 40 years.
Family history: Nothing in particular.
Past history: Pneumonia (age 32), diabetes (age 52), fractured clavicle (age 59).
Reason for detection: Sputum cytology mass survey revealed squamous cell carcinoma. Chest radiograph revealed no abnormality. (Tokyo Medical College Hospital)

**175**

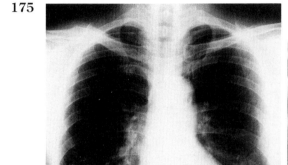

175 Chest radiograph appears normal.

**176**

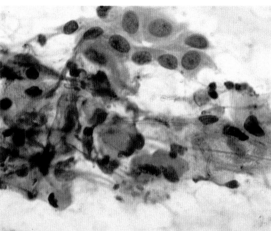

176 Brushing specimen reveals squamous cell carcinoma comprising a mixture of keratinized and non-keratinized cells (×400).

**177**

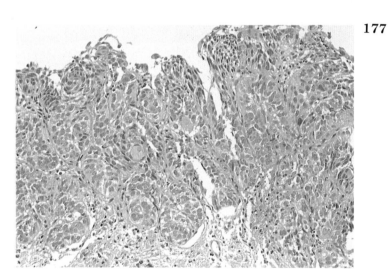

177 Biopsy specimen reveals squamous cell carcinoma with a small keratotic focus (×200).

## GRANULARITY — 5

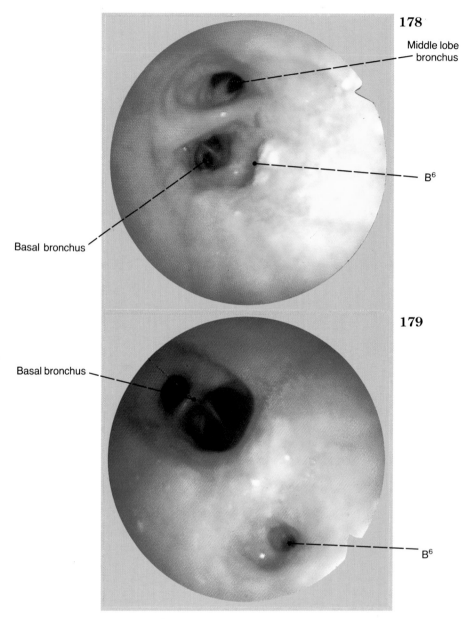

**178** Middle lobe bronchus

$B^6$

Basal bronchus

**179**

Basal bronchus

$B^6$

**178,179** Endoscopic findings from the right truncus intermedius to the right lower lobe show loss of the longitudinal folds in the truncus intermedius, loss of luster, and fine granularity, but there is almost no stenosis. There is also loss of luster of the bifurcation of the right basal bronchus and $B^6$, which was slightly stenotic.

*Patient:* 67-year-old male, garbage man who had been a farmer.
*Smoking history:* 15/day, 50 years.
*Family history:* Nothing in particular.
*Past history:* Laryngeal cancer (age 66).
*Reason for detection:* During follow-up for laryngeal cancer, productive cough developed and chest radiograph showed an abnormal shadow (which was actually a different small cell cancer of the lung) in the lung field and sputum cytology revealed squamous cell carcinoma. (*Osaka Habikino Hospital*)

**180**

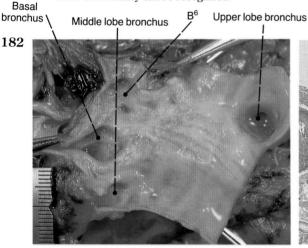

**180** Apart from the 1.2-cm diameter shadow in the right upper lung field (S$^1$), no other abnormality can be recognized.

**181**

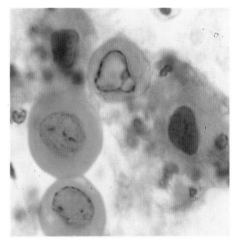

**181** Sputum cytology specimen reveals squamous cell carcinoma (×*1000*).

Basal bronchus \   Middle lobe bronchus   B$^6$   Upper lobe bronchus

**182**

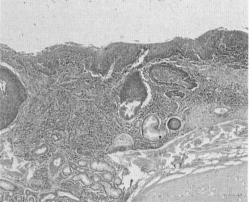

**182** Resected right lung reveals a superficially invading lesion that extends from the bifurcation of the truncus intermedius to the basal bronchus and B$^6$.

**183**

**183** Histological findings in the resected specimen reveal invasion of the duct of a bronchial gland by the superficially infiltrating squamous cell carcinoma. This was a case of triple primary cancer–laryngeal cancer, squamous cell carcinoma of the lung, and small cell carcinoma of the lung (×*40*).

## THICKENING AND SWELLING + GRANULARITY — 1

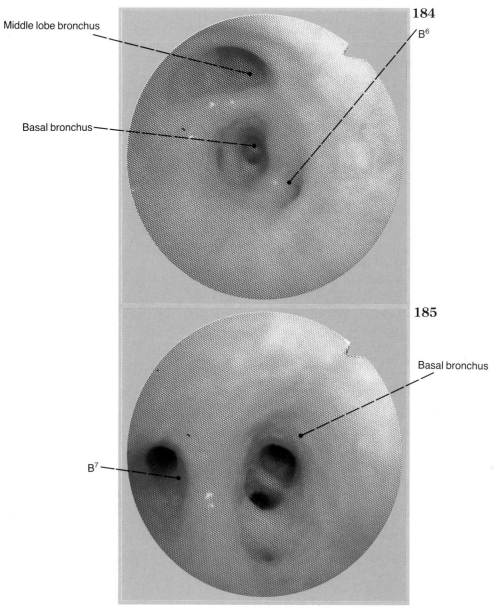

Middle lobe bronchus

**184**

B⁶

Basal bronchus

**185**

Basal bronchus

B⁷

**184, 185** Bifurcation of the right truncus intermedius and basal bronchus (**184**): bifurcation of the right middle lobe bronchus and that of B⁶ is thickened and reddened, and the mucosal folds have disappeared. The basal bronchus (**185**) shows small granular protrusions in the mucosa, redness, thickening of the bifurcation, and lack of definition or loss of mucosal folds can be recognized.

*Patient:* 54-year-old male, driver.
*Smoking history:* 20/day, 34 years.
*Family history:* Nothing in particular.
*Past history:* Gastric ulcer (age 34).
*Reason for detection:* Bloody sputum had appeared approximately 2 months previously and sputum cytology revealed squamous cell carcinoma. (*Kinki Central Hospital*)

**186**

**187**

**188**

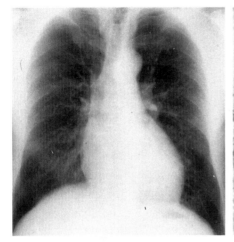

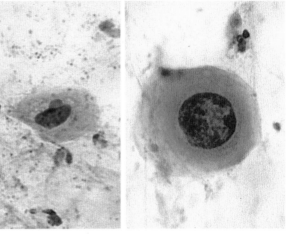

**186** Chest radiograph reveals no abnormality.

**187,188** Sputum cytology specimens demonstrate squamous cell carcinoma (×*1000*).

**189**

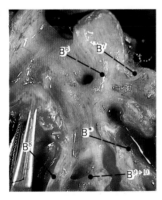

**189** Resected middle and lower bilobectomy specimen reveals thickening of the mucosa at the orifices of the right middle lobe and B⁶ and the mucosal folds are indistinct. Invasion was also recognized at the orifice of the anomalous

**190**

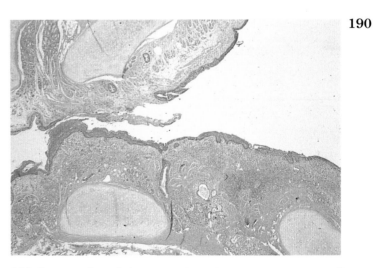

**190** Cross-section of the resected specimen at the orifice of B⁶ shows that almost all of the invasion is intraepithelial but tumor cells have replaced the duct of the bronchial gland.

B* The lesion covered an extensive area, from the orifice of B* to that of B⁶ and to the orifice of the middle lobe bronchus.

## THICKENING AND SWELLING + GRANULARITY — 2

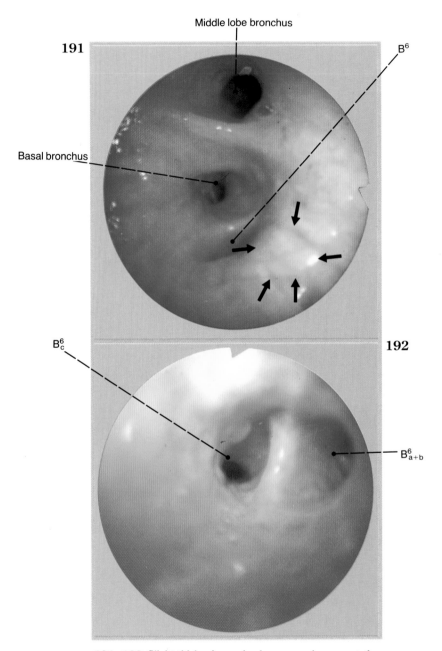

**191, 192** Slight thickening and paleness can be seen at the orifice of the right $B^6$ (**191**). Invasion extends from $B^6$ beyond the bifurcation of the subsegmental bronchi in the direction of $B_c^6$ (**192**). There is also irregular thickening and swelling.

*Patient:* 54-year-old male, company employee.
*Smoking history:* 30/day, 30 years.
*Family history:* Nothing in particular.
*Past history:* Nothing in particular.
*Reason for detection:* Sputum cytology carried out as part of an educational television postal survey revealed squamous cell carcinoma of the lung. Chest radiograph was normal. (*Tokyo Medical College Hospital*)

**193**

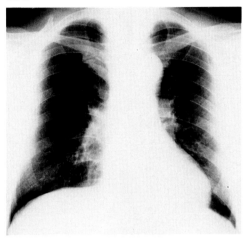

**193** Normal chest radiograph findings.

**194**

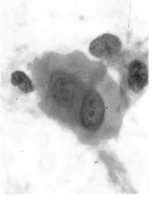

**194** Sputum cytology reveals small oval squamous carcinoma cells (×*400*).

**195**

**195** Brushing cytology shows small oval squamous carcinoma cells with a low degree of atypia (×*400*).

**196**

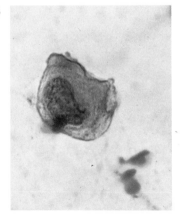

**196** Squamous carcinoma cell with a low degree of atypia obtained by brushing cytology (×*400).*

**197**

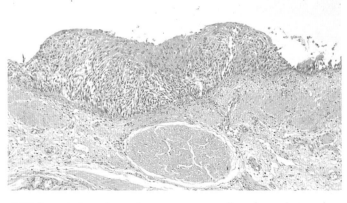

**197** Resected specimen shows squamous cell carcinoma but no clear submucosal invasion (×*40).*

# THICKENING AND SWELLING + GRANULARITY — 3

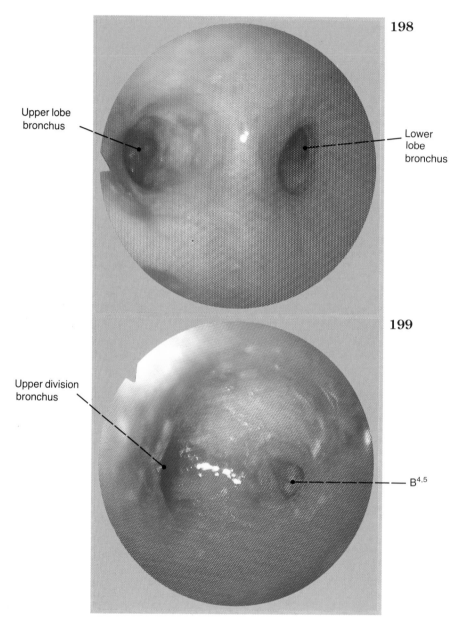

**Upper lobe bronchus**

**Lower lobe bronchus**

**198**

**199**

**Upper division bronchus**

**— B$^{4,5}$**

**198, 199** Bifurcation of left upper and lower lobe bronchi (**198**) and left upper lobe bronchus (**199**). The bifurcation of the left upper and lower lobe bronchi is thickened. The bifurcation of the lingular bronchus and the upper division bronchus bled easily and the upper division bronchus was stenotic. The lesion was a superficially invasive squamous cell carcinoma that extended from the lingular bronchus to the upper division bronchus.

**200**

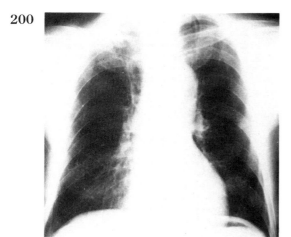

**200** Chest radiograph reveals nothing, apart from fibrosis.

**201**

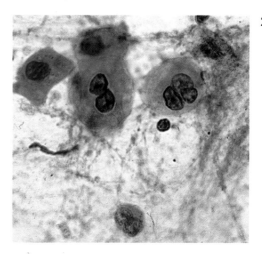

**201** Squamous carcinoma cells in the sputum specimen (×*400*).

**202**

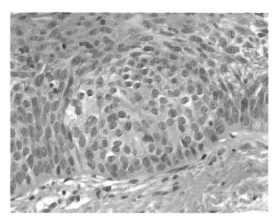

**202** Resected specimen reveals that the basal membrane was intact in parts (×*200*).

## THICKENING AND SWELLING + GRANULARITY — 4

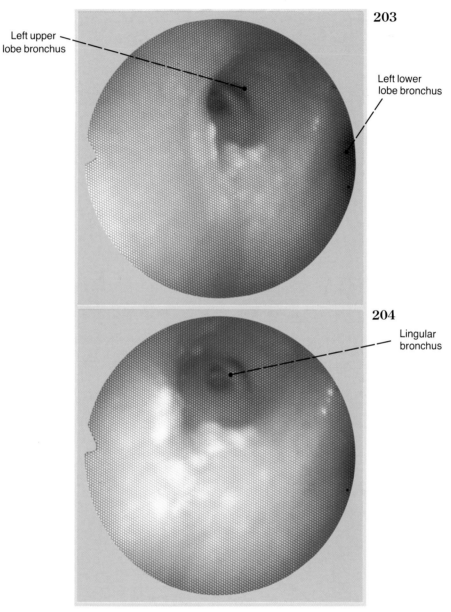

**203, 204** The orifice of the left upper lobe bronchus is pale, with a swollen granular surface. The lesion extends as far as the segmental bronchi.

*Patient:* 50-year-old male, company employee.
*Smoking history:* 40/day, 30 years.
*Family history:* Nothing in particular.
*Past history:* Nothing in particular.
*Reason for detection:* Detected by a postal sputum cytology survey. (*Tokyo Medical College Hospital*)

**205**

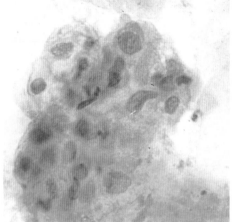

**205** Sputum cytology reveals a cluster of atypical cells that were difficult to distinguish from squamous carcinoma cells (×*400*).

**206**

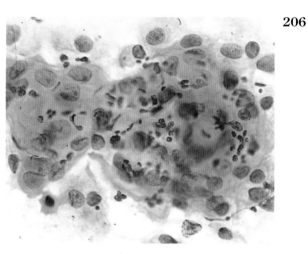

**206** Brushing cytology produces squamous carcinoma cells with a remarkable increase in chromatin (×*400*).

**207**

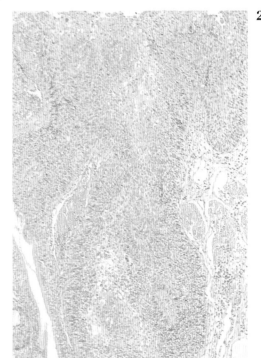

**207** Resected specimen reveals moderately differentiated squamous cell carcinoma, with distinct submucosal invasion extending to the distal side of the cartilage (×*40*).

# NODULARITY — 1

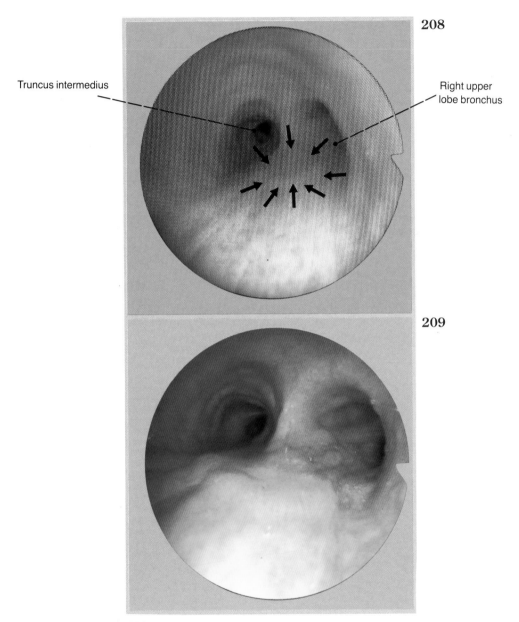

Truncus intermedius

Right upper
lobe bronchus

**208**

**209**

**208, 209** A slight flat elevation extends from the right
main bronchus to the right upper lobe bronchus (**208**). The
irregular lesion continues to the periphery of the right upper
lobe bronchus (**209**).

Patient: 60-year-old male, company employee.
Smoking history: 60/day, 40 years.
Family history: Elder sister had brain tumor.
Past history: Gastric ulcer (age 28).
Reason for detection: Cough and sputum. Chest radiograph was normal but sputum cytology revealed squamous cell carcinoma. (Tokyo Medical College Hospital)

**210**

**211**

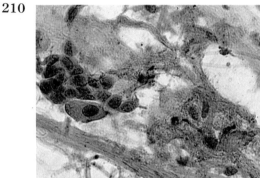

**210** Keratinized squamous carcinoma cells in sputum (×400).

**211** Brushing cytology gave a cluster of non-keratinized squamous carcinoma cells with remarkable increase of chromatin (×400).

**212**

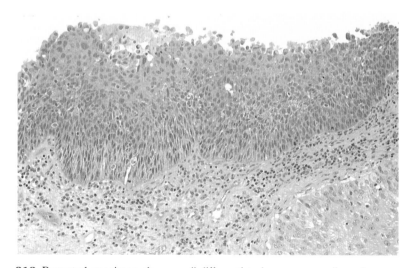

**212** Resected specimen shows well-differentiated squamous cell carcinoma. The basal membrane exhibits a wavy appearance that suggests submucosal invasion. On the lower right, distinct submucosal invasion can be seen (×100).

# NODULARITY – 2

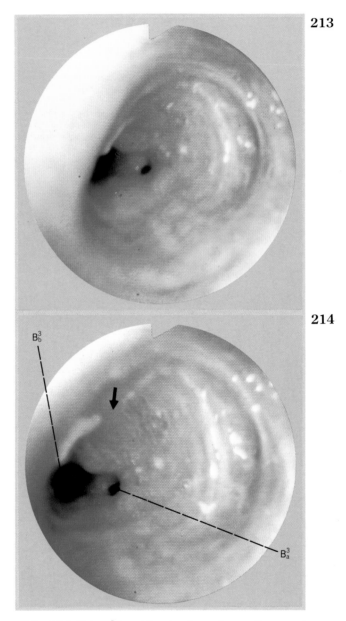

**213**

**214**

**213, 214** Right B$^3$ is reddened and granular, partly covered by a white coating, and both B$^3_a$ and B$^3_b$ are markedly stenotic.

> *Patient:* 68-year-old male, restaurant proprietor.
> *Smoking history:* 10/day, 48 years.
> *Family history:* Nothing in particular.
> *Past history:* Pulmonary tuberculosis (age 45), chronic hepatitis (age 60).
> *Reason for detection:* Cough and bloody sputum for 1 month previously. Sputum cytology in a lung cancer mass survey yielded a diagnosis of squamous cell carcinoma. Chest radiograph was normal. (*Center for Adult Diseases, Osaka*)

**215**

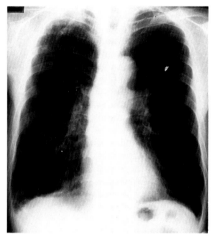

**215** Normal chest radiograph.

**216**

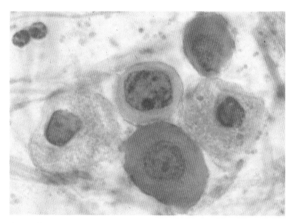

**216** Sputum cytology specimen treated by the mucolytic method (×*1000*).

**217**

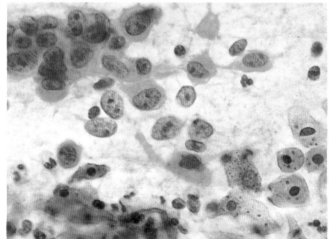

**217** Brushing cytology specimen from B³ (×*400*).

**218**

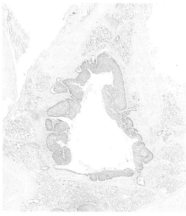

**218** Cross-section of B³ from the resected specimen reveals that the lesion extends almost completely around B³.

NODULARITY — 3

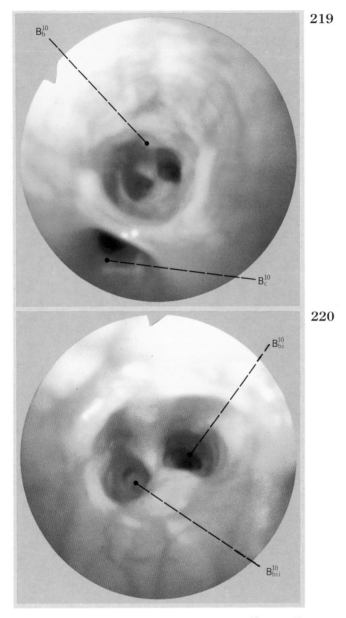

**219, 220** Thickening of the bifurcation of $B_{bi}^{10}$ and $B_{bii}^{10}$. There is a small protrusion proximal to the bifurcation and some submucosal blood vessels appear disrupted.

*Patient:* 58-year-old male, retired company employee.
*Smoking history:* 20/day, 32 years.
*Family history:* Nothing in particular.
*Past history:* Gastric ulcer (age 56), serum hepatitis (since age 56).
*Reason for detection:* Although asymptomatic he was classified as class D on a lung cancer mass survey and followed up. (*Osaka Habikino Hospital*)

**221**

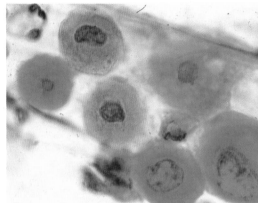

**222**

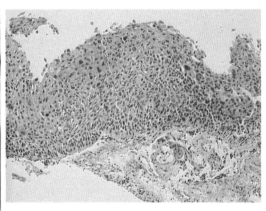

**222** Biopsy specimen indicates squamous cell carcinoma limited to within the epithelium (×*100*).

**221** Fresh sputum smear reveals squamous cell carcinoma (×*1000*).

**223**

**224**

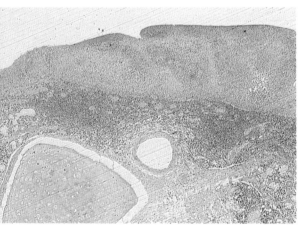

**223** Right lower lobectomy specimen reveals a small protrusion in $B_h^{10}$.

**224** Histological findings confirm that the squamous cell carcinoma lesion is limited to within the epithelium (×*40*).

# NODULARITY — 4

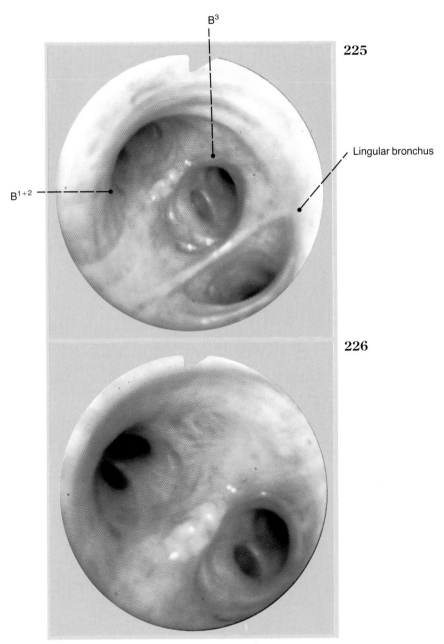

**225, 226** Uneven irregularity can be seen at the bifurcation of the left $B^{1+2}$ and $B^3$.

*Patient:* 66-year-old male, company employee.
*Smoking history:* 30/day, 46 years.
*Family history:* Brother died of lung cancer.
*Past history:* Appendicitis (age 20).
*Reason for detection:* Abnormal shadow detected on chest radiograph mass survey. Fiberoptic bronchoscopy revealed tumors at the orifice of right $B^2$ and at the bifurcation of the lingular bronchus and left upper division bronchus. Brushing cytology revealed the former to be small cell carcinoma and the latter to be squamous cell carcinoma. (*Center for Adult Diseases, Osaka*)

**227**

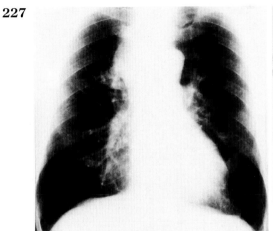

**228**

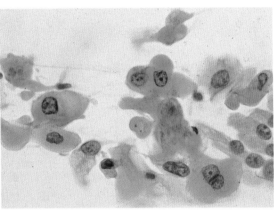

**228** Brushing cytology of the left $B^{1+2}$ and $B^3$ (×*400*).

**227** Chest radiograph reveals enlarged hilar and mediastinal shadows.

**229**

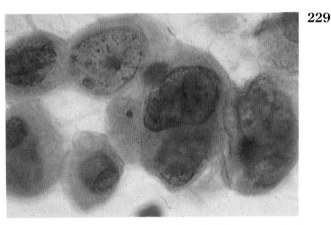

**229** Brushing cytology specimen from the bifurcation of left $B^{1+2}$ and $B^3$ (×*1000*).

NODULARITY — 5

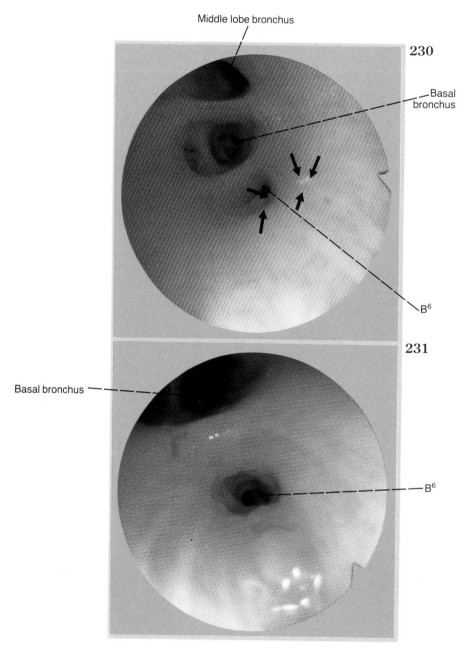

Middle lobe bronchus

230

Basal
bronchus

B⁶

231

Basal bronchus

B⁶

**230, 231** Protrusive edematous nodule in the lateral area of the bifurcation of right $B^6$ and irregular mucosa in the dorsolateral area of $B^6$.

*Patient:* 59-year-old female, unemployed.
*Smoking history:* 10–15/day, 25 years.
*Family history:* Nothing in particular.
*Past history:* Uterine myoma (age 33), gall bladder polyp (age 44).
*Reason for detection:* On a health checkup, the chest radiograph was normal but sputum cytology revealed squamous cell carcinoma. (*Tokyo Medical College Hospital*)

**232**

**232** Sputum cytology reveals non-keratotic squamous carcinoma cells (×*400*).

**233**
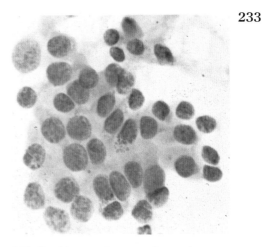

**233** Brushing cytology specimen shows a cluster of squamous carcinoma cells with relatively low atypia and increased chromatin (×*400*).

Middle lobe bronchus

Basal bronchus

**234**
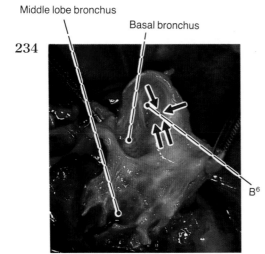

B⁶

**234** Resected specimen shows a small nodular tumor at the orifice of B⁶.

**235**
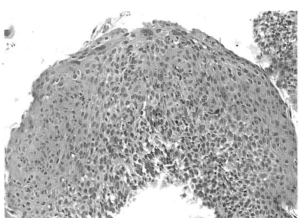

**235** Biopsy specimen shows moderately differentiated squamous cell carcinoma. This intraepithelial carcinoma did not extend beyond the basal membrane (×*100*).

# NODULARITY — 6

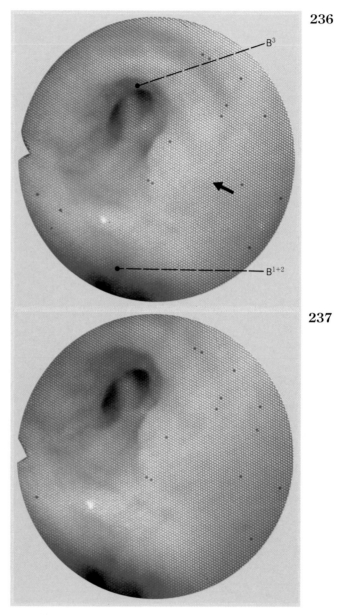

**236** B³

**236**

**237**

**B¹⁺²**

**236, 237** A small nodular protrusion with a slightly irregular surface is seen immediately proximal to the orifice of left B³.

*Patient:* 78-year-old male.
*Smoking history:* 20/day, 53 years.
*Past history:* Bronchial asthma (age 60).
*Reason for detection:* Bloody sputum for several days 1 month previously. Chest radiograph was normal but sputum cytology yielded a diagnosis of squamous cell carcinoma. (*Center for Adult Diseases, Osaka*)

**238**  **239**  **240**

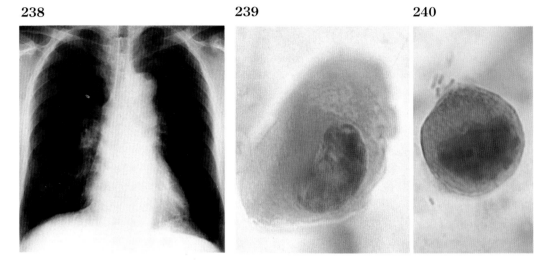

**238** Normal chest radiograph.

**239, 240** Keratinized cells with large irregular nuclei are recognized by sputum cytology (×*1000*).

**241**

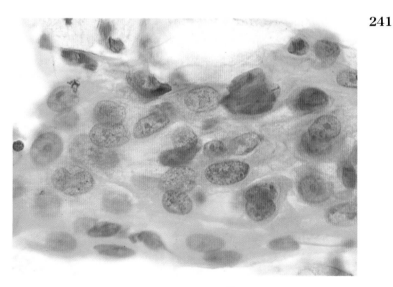

**241** Brushing cytology of the tumor in left B$^3$ (×*400*).

**NODULARITY — 7**

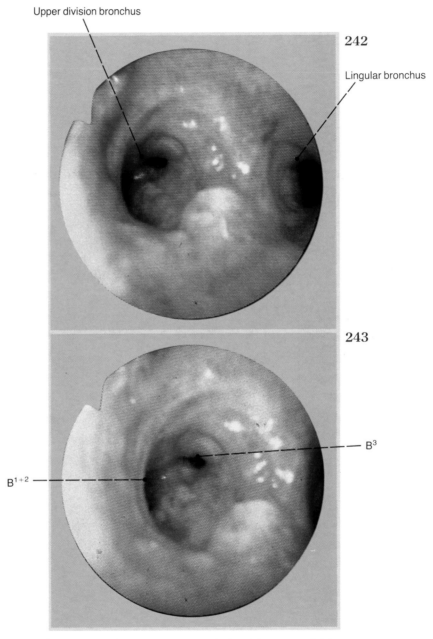

**242, 243** Irregular mucosa of the left upper division bronchus and a small nodule at the orifice are recognizable, while $B^{1+2}$ and $B^3$ are stenotic.

*Patient:* 78-year-old male, unemployed.
*Smoking history:* 30/day, 50 years.
*Family history:* Nothing in particular.
*Past history:* Pleuritis (age 10), pulmonary tuberculosis (age 32), cerebral infarction (age 72).
*Reason for detection:* Bloody sputum from 1 month previously prompted a checkup. Chest radiograph revealed no abnormality but sputum cytology yielded a diagnosis of squamous cell carcinoma. (*Center for Adult Diseases, Osaka*)

**244**

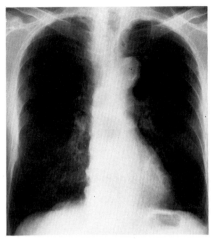

**244** Chest radiograph does not show any distinct abnormality.

**245**

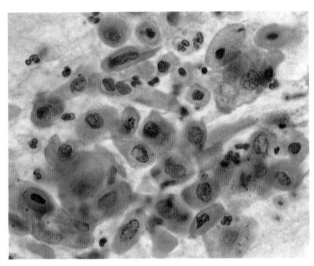

**245** Brushing cytology specimen (×*400*).

**246**

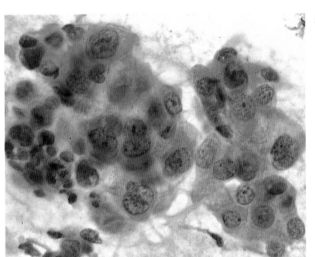

**246** Brushing cytology specimen (×*400*).

# NODULARITY — 8

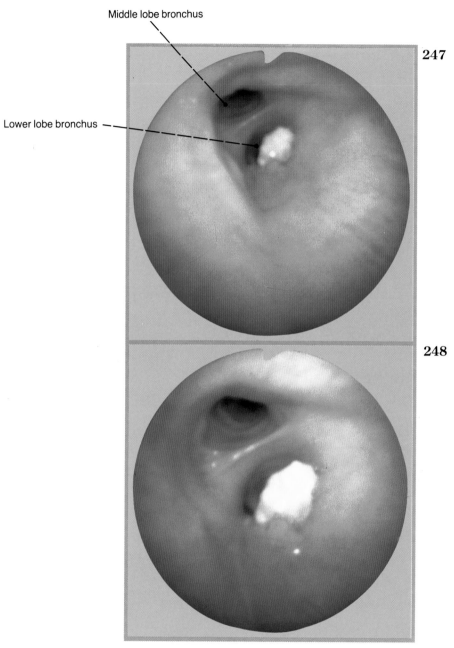

Middle lobe bronchus

Lower lobe bronchus

**247**

**248**

**247, 248** A tumor covered with a white coating protrudes from B$^6$ into the right lower lobe bronchus.

*Patient:* 68-year-old male, farmer.
*Smoking history:* 30/day, 50 years.
*Family history:* Brother had gastric cancer.
*Past history:* Peritonitis (age 34).
*Reason for detection:* An abnormal shadow was detected on a lung cancer checkup and the results of sputum cytology were class E. (*Osaka Habikino Hospital*)

**249**

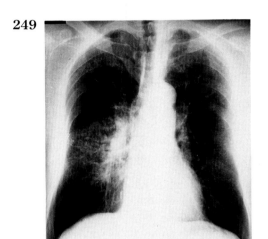

**250**

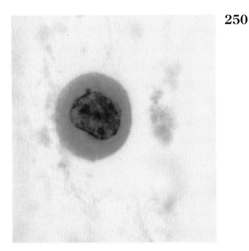

**249** An infiltrative shadow is recognized in the right middle lung field. Lateral tomograms revealed obstructive pneumonia in S⁶.

**250** A squamous carcinoma cell is recognized in a fresh sputum specimen (×1000).

**251**

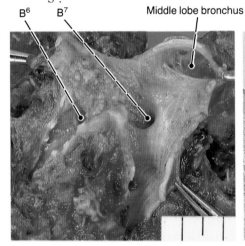

**252**

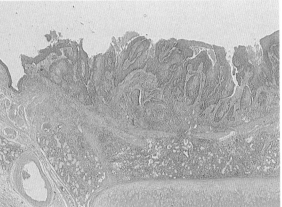

**251** Resected specimen shows an invasive polyp at the orifice of B⁶.

**252** Histological findings of the resected specimen show an infiltrative polyp, with invasion as far as the outer layer of the bronchial wall (×40).

# NODULARITY — 9

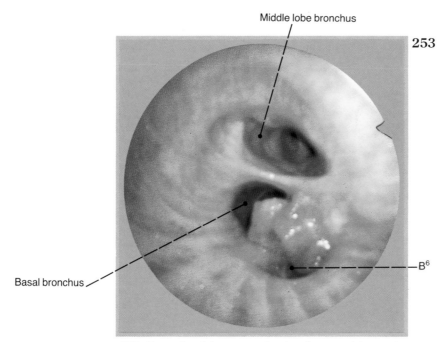

**253** From the right truncus intermedius a nodule can be seen protruding from the bifurcation of $B^6$ and the basal bronchus.

Patient: 62-year-old male, restaurant worker.
Smoking history: 30/day, 42 years.
Family history: Nothing in particular.
Past history: Right pleuritis (age 41).
Reason for detection: Bloody sputum had appeared intermittently for almost 2 years but its frequency had increased during the past month. (Osaka Habikino Hospital)

**254**

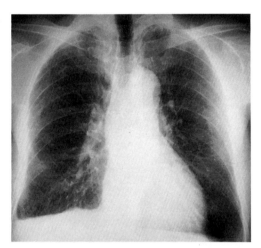

**254** Chest radiograph reveals no abnormal finding apart from right pleural thickening.

**255**

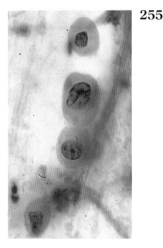

**255** Sputum cytology shows squamous cell carcinoma (×400).

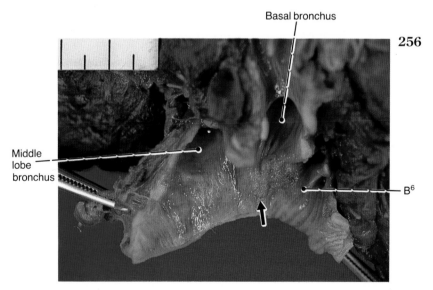

**256** The resected specimen shows an invasive polyp (arrow) at the bifurcation of B⁶ and the basal bronchus.

# NODULARITY — 10

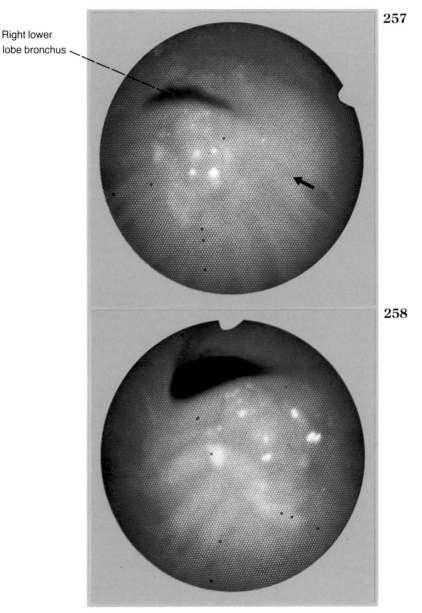

Right lower
lobe bronchus

**257**

**258**

**257, 258** Multiple nodules can be seen protruding at the
orifice of the right lower lobe bronchus.

*Patient:* 63-year-old male, company employee.
*Smoking history:* 20/day, 35 years.
*Family history:* Father died of lung cancer at age 77.
*Past history:* High blood pressure (age 60), diabetes (age 63).
*Reason for detection:* Cough and continuous sputum developed 10 months previously.
He underwent bronchoscopy due to a pneumonia-like shadow that had developed 1
month previously in S$^6$. (*Center for Adult Diseases, Osaka*)

**259**

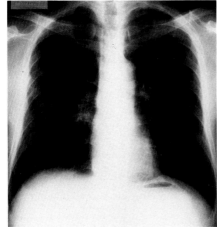

**260**

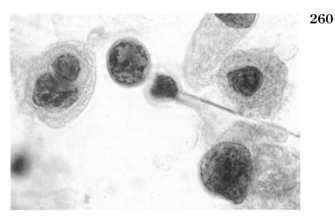

**260** Sputum cytology specimen (×*1000*).

**259** Chest radiograph reveals a slight shadow in S$^6$.

Truncus intermedius

Middle
lobe bronchus

**261**

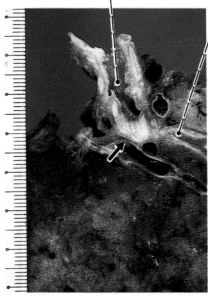

**262**

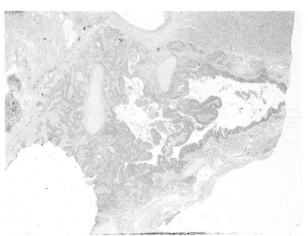

**261** Resected specimen shows a tumor (arrow) almost obstructing the right basal bronchus.

**262** Cross-section of the resected specimen shows squamous cell carcinoma.

# NODULARITY — 11

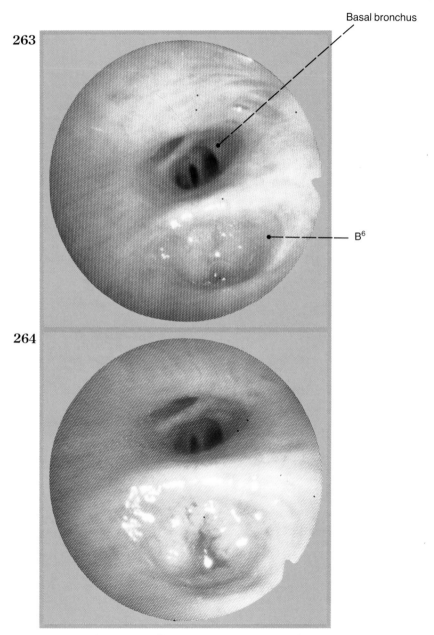

**263, 264** The right B$^6$ is obstructed by a polypoid tumor with an edematous, partly transparent surface. The tumor compresses the basal bronchus and the bifurcation, and mucosal thickening can be observed.

*Patient:* 71-year-old male, unemployed.
*Smoking history:* 20/day, 30 years.
*Family history:* Nothing in particular.
*Reason for detection:* On a regular health checkup, chest radiograph was negative but sputum cytology yielded a diagnosis of squamous cell carcinoma. (*Tokyo Medical College Hospital*)

**265**

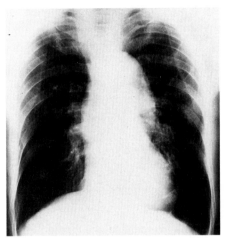

**265** Chest radiograph reveals no abnormal findings.

**266**

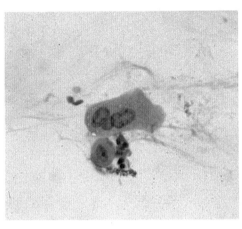

**266** Keratotic squamous carcinoma cell in sputum (×*400*).

**267**

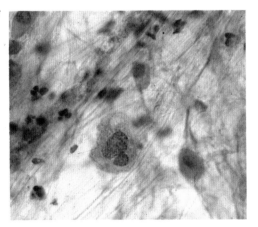

**267** Another keratotic squamous carcinoma cell in sputum (×*400*).

**268**

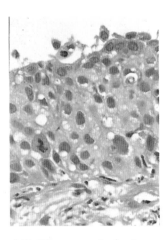

**268** Biopsy specimen demonstrates squamous cell carcinoma (×*200*).

NODULARITY — 12

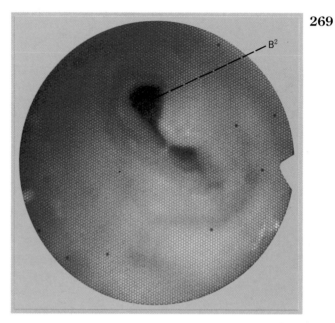

269

**269** A small nodule can be seen at the orifice of right $B^2$.

*Patient:* 69-year-old male, fish wholesaler.
*Smoking history:* 10/day, 50 years.
*Family history:* Nothing in particular.
*Past history:* Acute pneumonitis (age 29), angina pectoris (age 57), gout (age 68).
*Reason for detection:* Cough and sputum had appeared 1 month previously. He also suffered several asthmatic attacks. Chest radiograph was negative but sputum cytology revealed squamous cell carcinoma. (*Hokkaido University*)

**270**

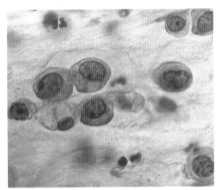

**270** Squamous carcinoma cells in the sputum specimen (×*400*).

**271**

**271** Brushing specimen also reveals squamous cell carcinoma (×*400*).

**272**

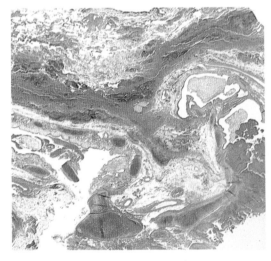

**272** Resected specimen shows that it is an early stage lesion that has not gone beyond the bronchial cartilage.

**273**

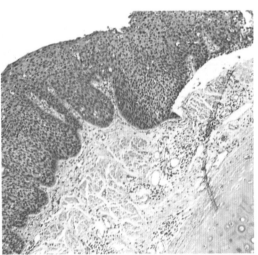

**273** Histological appearance of the resected tumor (×*40*).

**NODULARITY — 13**

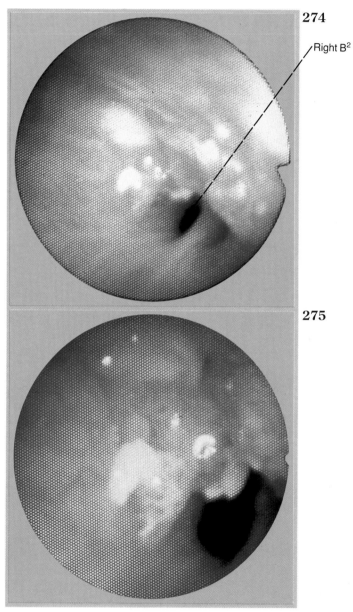

**274**

Right B$^2$

**275**

**274, 275** Anterior wall of the right upper lobe bronchus shows reddening and swelling and some areas covered by a white coating, which is also seen at the orifice of B$^3$. B$^3$ is partly obstructed by an irregularly surfaced invasive nodule.

*Patient:* 57-year-old male.
*Smoking history:* 20/day, 37 years.
*Past history:* Cerebral infarction (age 53).
*Reason for detection:* An abnormal shadow was detected on radiography when he consulted his local physician due to a troublesome cough that had developed 2 months previously; sputum cytology yielded a diagnosis of squamous cell carcinoma.
*(Center for Adult Diseases, Osaka)*

**276**

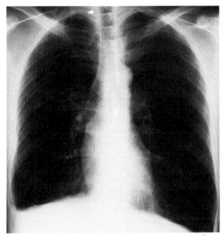

**277**

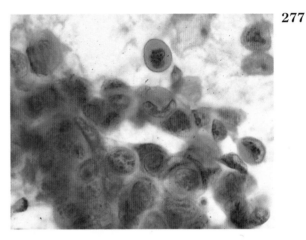

**277** Brushing cytology specimen (×*400*).

**276** Infiltrative shadow seen in $S^2$ began to disappear on administration of antibiotics.

**278**

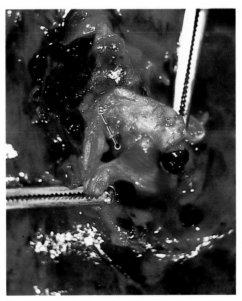

**278** Resected specimen reveals an invasive nodule at the orifice of right $B^3$.

**NODULARITY — 14**

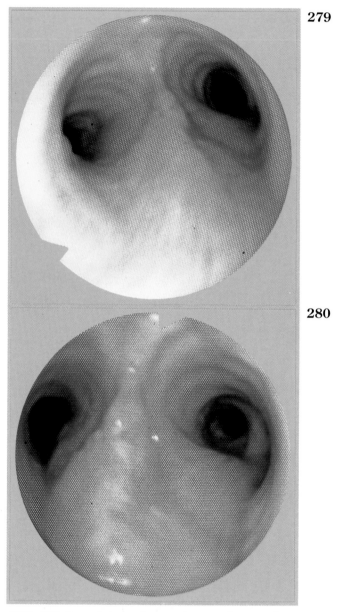

**279, 280** Irregularity and protrusions can be seen from the membranous portion of the lower trachea to the carina. The mucosa shows redness and granularity in parts.

*Patient:* 54-year-old male, seaweed processor.
*Smoking history:* 40/day, 34 years.
*Family history:* Nothing in particular.
*Past history:* Pleuritis (age 6), pneumonia (age 46).
*Reason for detection:* Occasional bloody sputum had occurred for 10 months. Chest radiograph revealed no abnormalities, but fiberoptic bronchoscopy showed a tumor at the carina and biopsy yielded a diagnosis of squamous cell carcinoma. (*Center for Adult Diseases, Osaka*)

**281**

**282**
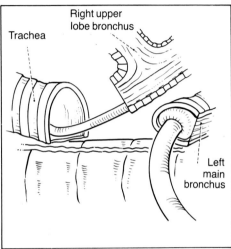

**281, 282** After resection of the carina, end-to-end anastomosis of the trachea and right main bronchus, and end-to-side anastomosis of the right main bronchus and left main bronchus were performed, with omental wrapping.

**283**
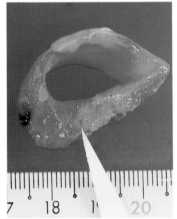

**284**
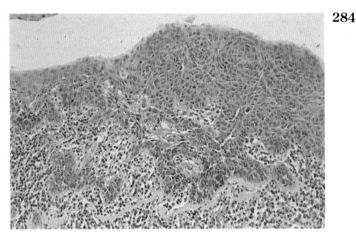

**283** Resected tumor extending from the membranous portion of the trachea to the carina.

**284** Histological findings in the resected specimen show that the submucosal invasion did not extend extramurally (×*100*).

## THICKENING AND SWELLING + NODULARITY — 1

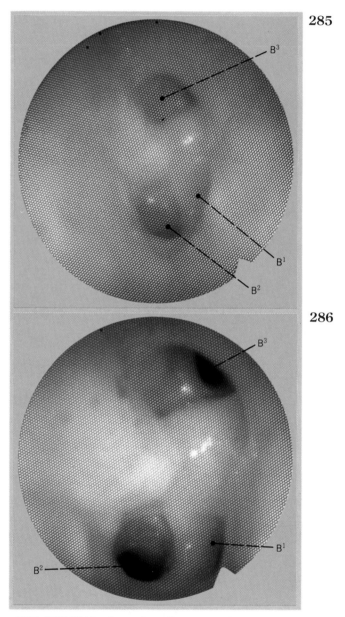

**285, 286** Thickening and swelling extend from the orifice of the right upper lobe bronchus to $B^1$, $B^2$, and $B^3$.

Patient: 59-year-old female, unemployed.
Smoking history: 10/day, 40 years.
Family history: Nothing in particular.
Past history: Acute pneumonitis (age 55), thyrotoxicosis (age 55), cataract (age 55).
Reason for detection: She developed a cough 1 month previously. Endoscopy and sputum cytology yielded a diagnosis of squamous cell carcinoma. Chest radiograph was normal. (Tokyo Medical College Hospital)

**287**

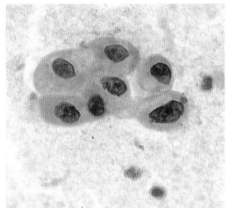

**287** Squamous carcinoma cells in the sputum specimen reveal increased chromatin (×400).

**288**

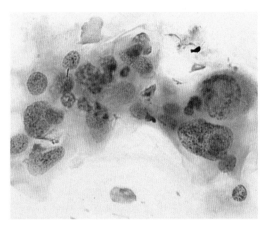

**288** Squamous carcinoma cells in the sputum show irregularity in size (×400).

**290**

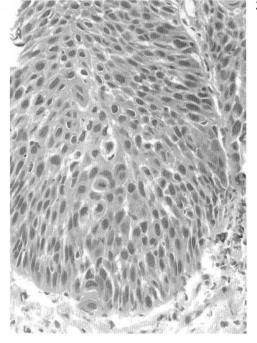

**289**

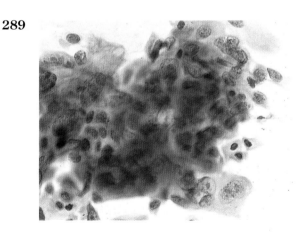

**289** Brushing cytology specimen shows a cluster of tumor cells containing multiple nucleoli (×400).

**290** Biopsy specimen shows the intraepithelial tumor (×200).

# THICKENING AND SWELLING + NODULARITY — 2

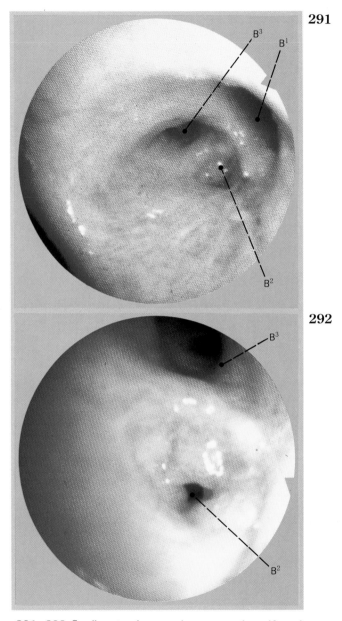

**291**

**292**

**291, 292** Small protrusions can be seen at the orifice of right $B^2$, with findings suggestive of superficial invasion extending to $B^1$ and $B^3$.

Patient: 60-year-old male, civil servant.
Smoking history: 20/day, 42 years.
Family history: Nothing in particular.
Past history: Pulmonary hilar lymphadenitis and pleuritis (age 19), hypertension (age 60).
Reason for detection: Regular health checkup. Sputum showed carcinoma cells. Chest radiograph revealed no abnormality apart from old pleuritis.
(Hokkaido University)

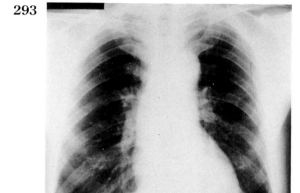

293 Chest radiograph shows obliteration of the left costophrenic angle and pleural thickening. There is no abnormality in the lung field.

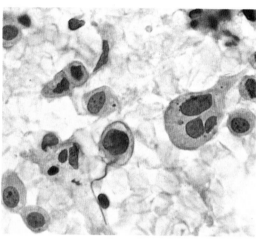

294 Sputum specimen shows squamous cell carcinoma (×400).

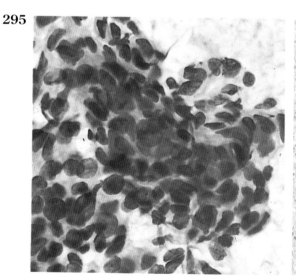

295 Brushing specimen shows squamous cell carcinoma (×400).

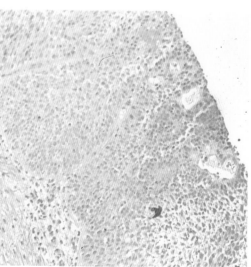

296 Histological findings of the resected specimen show the squamous cell carcinoma to be limited to within the epithelium (×100).

# THICKENING AND SWELLING + NODULARITY − 3

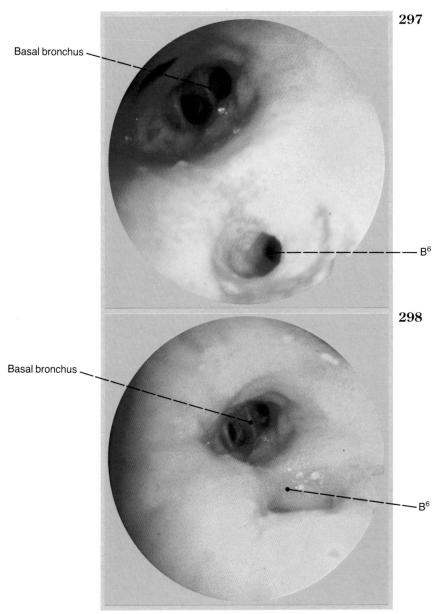

**297**

Basal bronchus

B⁶

**298**

Basal bronchus

B⁶

**297, 298** Irregular mucosa and findings suggestive of superficial infiltration can be seen at the orifice of right $B^6$.

Patient: 74-year-old male, unemployed.
Smoking history: 15/day, 56 years.
Family history: Nothing in particular.
Past history: Cataract (age 74).
Reason for detection: Asymptomatic. He had worked in a chromium factory for 18 years, from 1945–1963. He participated in a mass survey and sputum cytology revealed squamous cell carcinoma. (Hokkaido University).

**299**
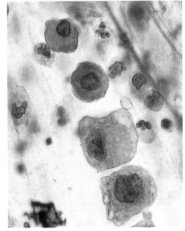

**300**
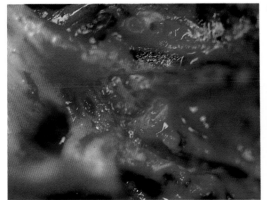

**299** Squamous carcinoma cells in sputum (×400).

**300** Brushing specimen shows squamous cell carcinoma (×400).

**301**
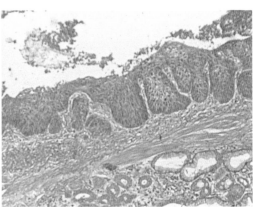

**302**

**301** Resected specimen.

**302** Histological findings of the resected specimen show the squamous cell carcinoma to be limited to within the epithelium (×40).

**THICKENING AND SWELLING + NODULARITY — 4**

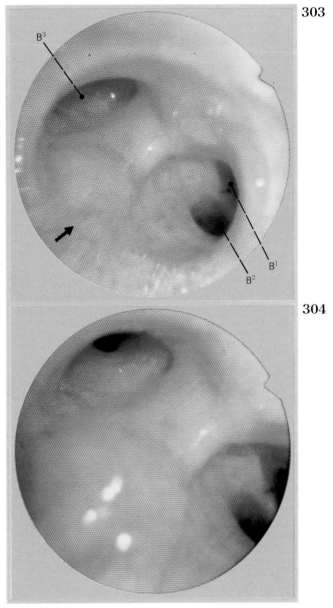

**303, 304** The right upper lobe bronchus bifurcated to $B^{1+2}$ and $B^3$, at which site a small protrusion with a smooth partially irregular surface was observed.

*Patient:* 66-year-old male, welder.
*Smoking history:* 20/day, 46 years.
*Family history:* Nothing in particular.
*Past history:* Bronchial asthma (age 65).
*Reason for detection:* Under treatment and follow-up for bronchial asthma by a local physician, increase of the left hilar shadow was noted. Fiberoptic bronchoscopy revealed a small nodule at the bifurcation of segmental bronchi in the right upper lobe bronchus and a tumor in left $B^6$. Brushing cytology revealed both to be squamous cell carcinoma, and advanced disease was recognized in the left lower lobe. (*Center for Adult Diseases, Osaka*)

**305**
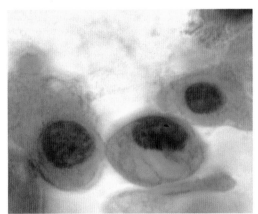

**306**
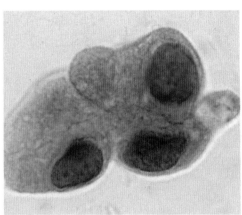

**305, 306** Sputum cytology specimens (×*1000*).

**307**
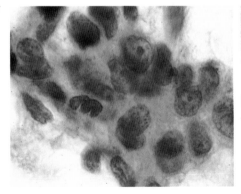

**307** Brushing cytology specimen from the lesion in the right upper lobe bronchus (×*1000*).

**308**
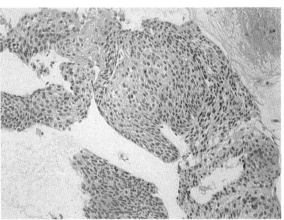

**308** Biopsy specimen from the right upper lobe bronchus showing squamous cell carcinoma (×*100*).

# THICKENING AND SWELLING + NODULARITY — 5

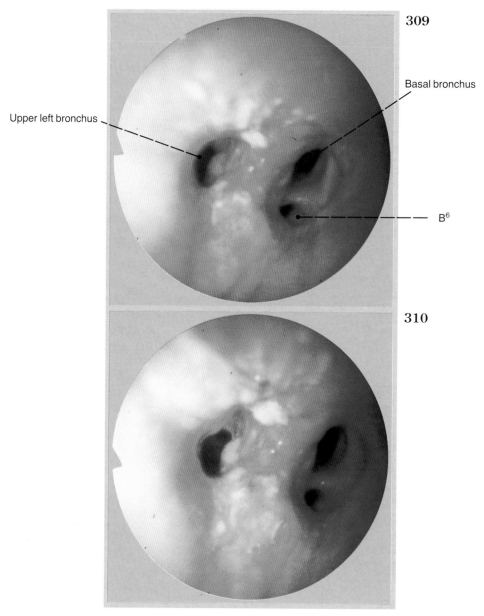

**309**

Basal bronchus

Upper left bronchus

B⁶

**310**

**309, 310** The bifurcation of the left upper and lower division bronchi is blunt and red, the mucosa is irregular and in parts there is adherent white material. Both orifices are stenotic, but more distally in the lower division bronchus there appears to be no stenosis.

Patient: 71-year-old female.
Smoking history: 5/day, 40 years.
Past history: Nothing in particular.
Reason for detection: Cough had developed 6 months previously and became more severe. Chest radiograph was normal but squamous carcinoma cells were detected by sputum cytology. (Center for Adult Diseases, Osaka)

311

312

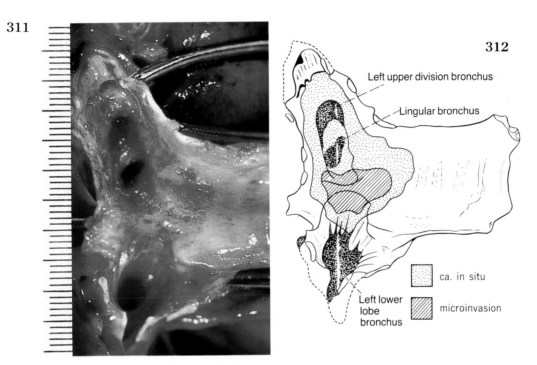

Left upper division bronchus

Lingular bronchus

ca. in situ

microinvasion

Left lower lobe bronchus

**311, 312** Resected specimen shows superficial invasion centered upon the bifurcation of the left upper and lower division (lingular) bronchi, with swelling and nodular formation.

313

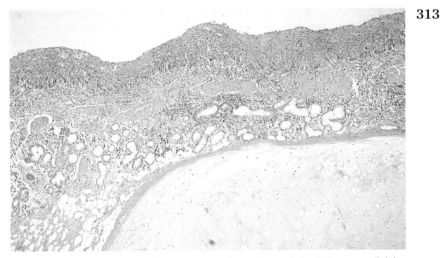

**313** Histological findings of the tumor at the orifice of the left upper division bronchus show most of the lesion to be intraepithelial, with some areas of microinvasion of well-differentiated squamous cell carcinoma (×40).

# THICKENING AND SWELLING + NODULARITY — 6

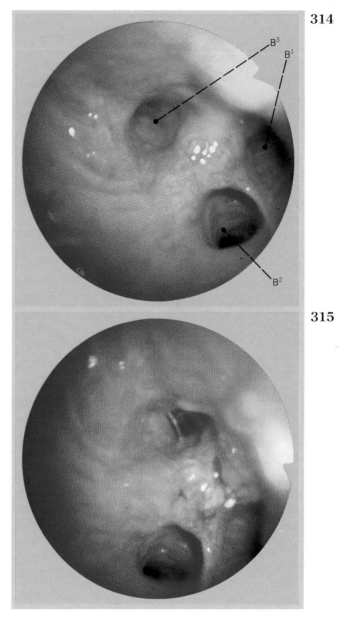

**314, 315** Superficial invasion at the bifurcation of right $B^2$ and $B^3$ shows an irregularly thickened surface.

*Patient:* 73-year-old male, unemployed.
*Smoking history:* 10/day, 56 years.
*Family history:* Nothing in particular.
*Past history:* Pleurisy (age 13), pancreatitis (age 58), angina pectoris (age 72).
*Reason for detection:* Developed symptoms of a common cold 2 months previously but cough and sputum did not abate. Sputum cytology by his local physician revealed atypical cells so he was followed up. (*Hokkaido University*)

**316**

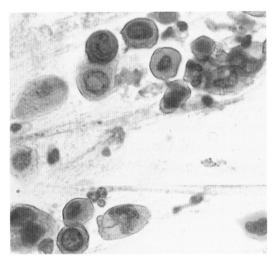

**316** Sputum specimen shows squamous carcinoma cells (×*400*).

**317**

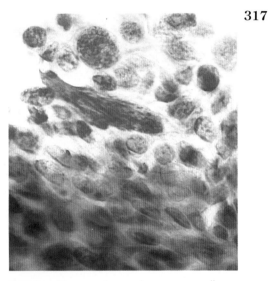

**317** Brushing specimen of squamous cell carcinoma (×*400*).

**319**

**318**

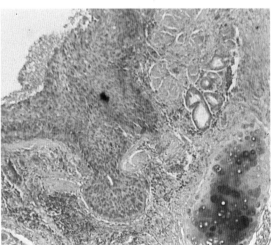

**318** Resected specimen.

**319** Histological findings show that the squamous cell carcinoma has not extended beyond the bronchial cartilage (×*100*).

## THICKENING AND SWELLING + NODULARITY — 7

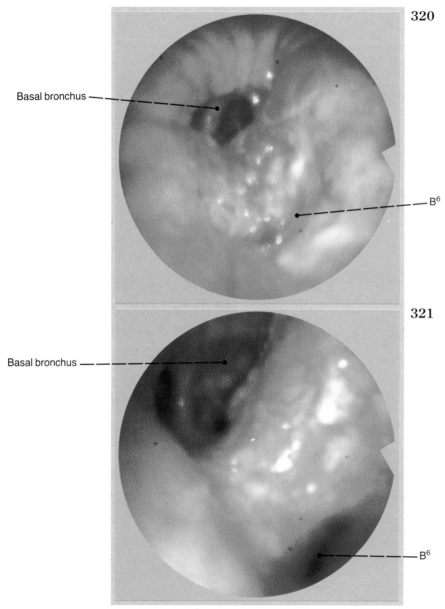

**320, 321** The mucosa at the orifice of right B[6], which is stenotic, is irregular and bleeds easily.

*Patient:* 56-year-old male, company employee.
*Smoking history:* 30/day, 30 years.
*Family history:* Nothing in particular.
*Past history:* Duodenal ulcers (age 27 and 55), herniated disk (age 37), hypertension (age 55).
*Reason for detection:* He presented with a history of fever and bloody sputum for 2 months. No abnormality was seen on chest radiograph. Squamous cell carcinoma was detected by sputum cytology. (*Tokyo Medical College Hospital*)

**322**

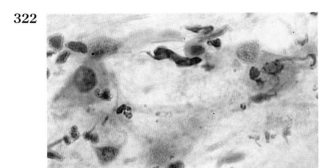

**323**

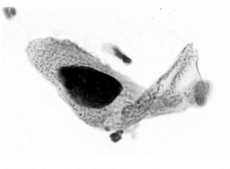

**323** A keratinized cell from the sputum, with remarkable increase in chromatin (×*1000*).

**322** Sputum cytology reveals keratinized squamous cell carcinoma (×*400*).

**324**

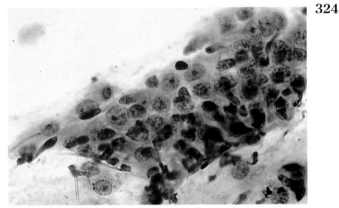

**324** Brushing cytology shows a cluster of cells with remarkable nucleoli (×*400*).

**325**

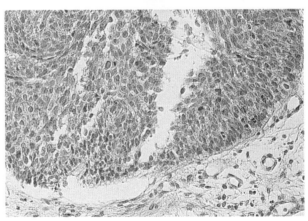

**325** Biopsy specimen showing basal cell type of intraepithelial carcinoma (×*100*).

# THICKENING AND SWELLING + NODULARITY — 8

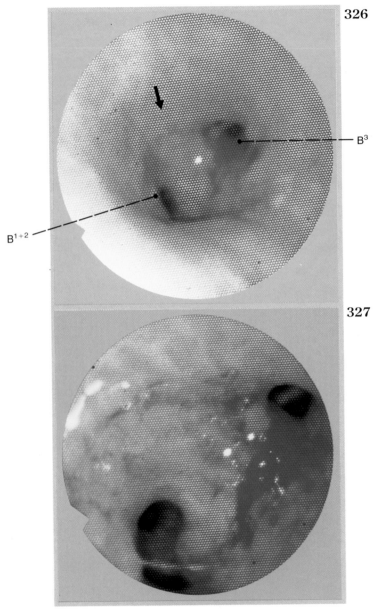

**326, 327** The bifurcation of left $B^{1+2}$ and $B^3$ shows remarkable redness and swelling, and mucosa has been replaced by irregular nodular invasion accompanied in some parts by bleeding.

*Patient:* 76-year-old male.
*Smoking history:* 30/day, 50 years.
*Past history:* Thyroid cancer (age 73), cancer of the bladder (age 74).
*Reason for detection:* Bloody sputum had appeared 3 months previously and sputum cytology revealed squamous cell carcinoma. (*Center for Adult Diseases, Osaka*)

**328** **329** **330**

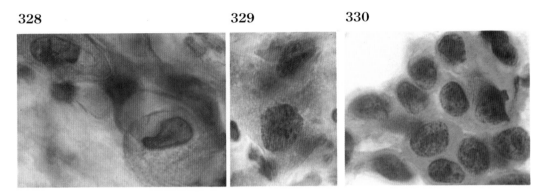

**328, 329** Sputum cytology specimens (×*1000*).

**330** Brushing cytology specimen (×*1000*).

**331**

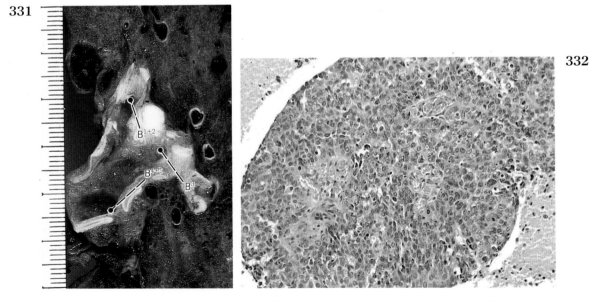

**332**

**331** Tumor with nodular invasion can be seen at the bifurcation of left $B^{1+2}$ and $B^3$.

**332** Histological findings of the resected specimen show squamous cell carcinoma (×*100*).

# THICKENING AND SWELLING + NODULARITY — 9

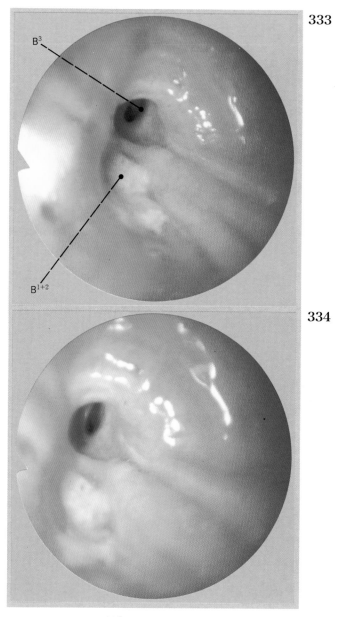

**333, 334** Left $B^{1+2}$ is obstructed by a tumor with a granular, edematous surface. Fusion of the membranous folds can be seen.

*Patient:* 74-year-old male, unemployed.
*Smoking history:* 20/day, 50 years.
*Family history:* Nothing in particular.
*Reason for detection:* Cough and sputum had continued for 6 months. Sputum cytology by his local physician revealed squamous cell carcinoma. (*Tokyo Medical College Hospital*)

**335**

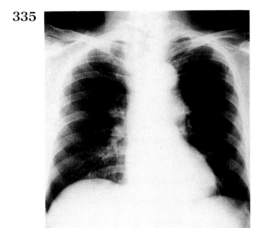

**336**

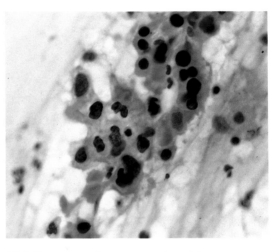

**335** Chest radiograph reveals no abnormality.

**336** Sputum specimen reveals keratinized squamous carcinoma cells (×*400*).

**337**

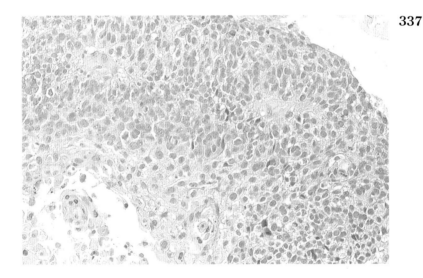

**337** Biopsy specimen shows moderately differentiated squamous cell carcinoma (×*200*).

## THICKENING AND SWELLING + NODULARITY — 10

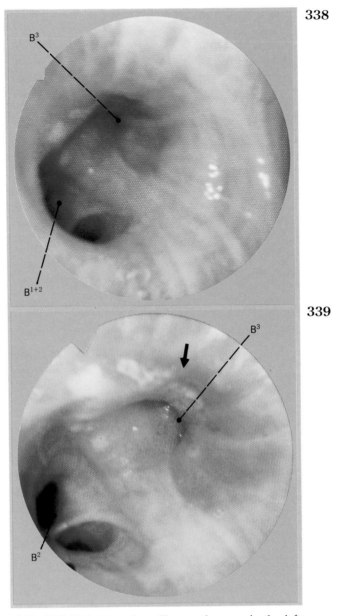

**338**

**339**

**338, 339** Redness and swelling can be seen in the left upper division bronchus, especially in B$^3$, which is also markedly stenotic, and adhesion of white material can be seen in areas.

*Patient:* 68-year-old male, unemployed.
*Smoking history:* 80/day, 48 years.
*Family history:* Nothing in particular.
*Reason for detection:* Bloody sputum for a month. Chest radiograph was unremarkable, but sputum cytology revealed squamous cell carcinoma. (*Center for Adult Diseases, Osaka*)

**340**      **341**      **342**

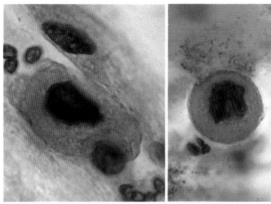

**340, 341** Sputum cytology specimens (×*1000*).

**342** Resected specimen shows the tumor extending like a tree in left B$^3$.

**343**

**343** Low-power magnification of the cross-section of left B$^3$ shows the tumor in the bronchial lumen, but there appears to be no extension beyond the bronchial wall.

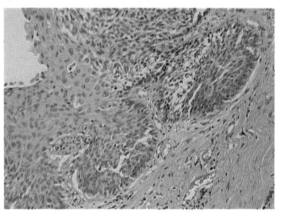

**344**

**344** Histological appearance of the tumor (×*100*).

POLYPS – 1

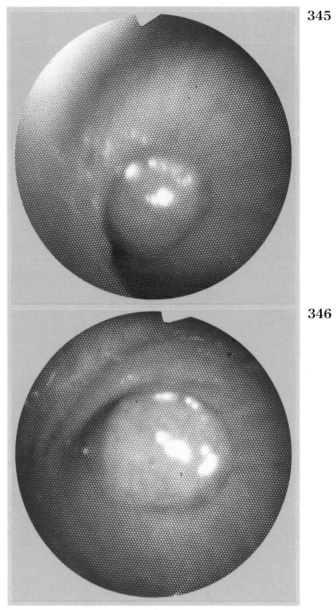

**345, 346** A polypoid tumor can be seen at the distal portion of the truncus intermedius. The surface is smooth and glossy. Capillaries are engorged.

*Patient:* 70-year-old male, printer.
*Smoking history:* 25/day, 23 years.
*Past history:* Hypertension (age 65), diabetes (age 69).
*Reason for detection:* Bloody sputum had appeared 2 weeks earlier and sputum cytology performed by his local physician revealed squamous cell carcinoma. (*Center for Adult Diseases, Osaka*)

**347**

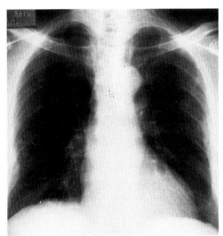

**347** Chest radiograph shows no remarkable abnormalities.

**348**

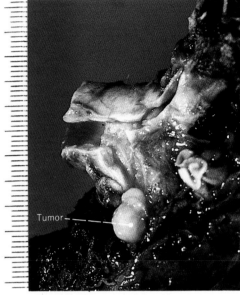

**348** Opening the truncus intermedius from the posterior aspect, the polypoid tumor protrudes into the truncus intermedius from the basal bronchus.

**349**

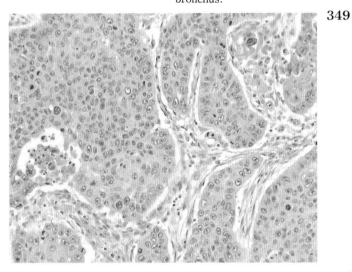

**349** Histological findings show primarily endobronchial development of moderately differentiated squamous cell carcinoma, partially invading the cartilage but limited to the bronchial wall (×*100*).

**POLYPS — 2**

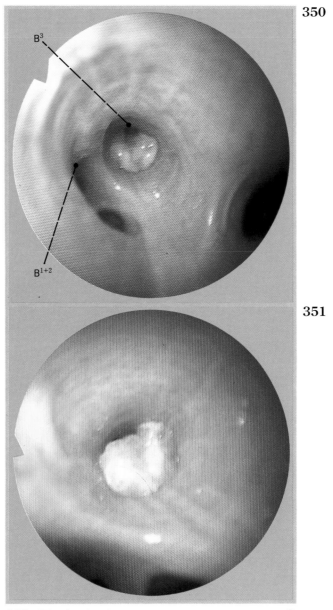

**350**

**351**

**350, 351** A polypoid lesion can be recognized in left B³ (**350**). Granular edematous changes can be seen but there is apparently no invasion in the surrounding bronchial wall. White material is also present (**351**).

Patient: 64-year-old male, company employee.
Smoking history: 20/day, 40 years.
Family history: Nothing in particular.
Reason for detection: Detected by sputum cytology in a mass survey. The chest radiograph was normal. (Tokyo Medical College Hospital)

**352**

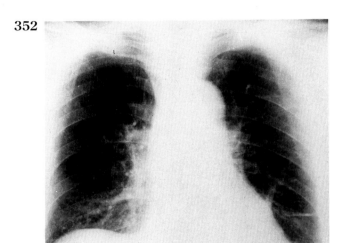

**353**

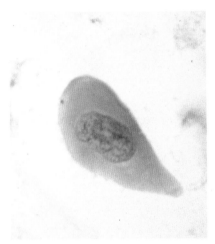

**352** Chest radiograph shows no abnormalities.

**353** Keratinized squamous cell found in sputum (×1000).

**354** Brushing cytology gave large squamous carcinoma cells with keratinized cytoplasm (×400).

**355**

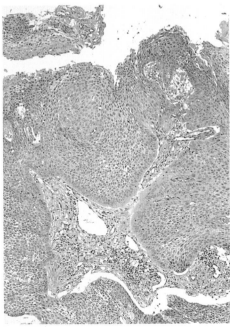

**355** Biopsy specimen shows the squamous cell carcinoma to have formed a polyp consisting primarily of squamous carcinoma cells on its surface. Submucosal invasion cannot be seen (×40).

**354**

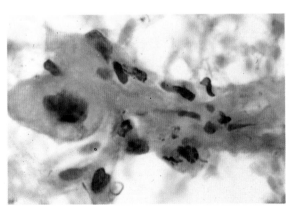

## POLYPS – 3

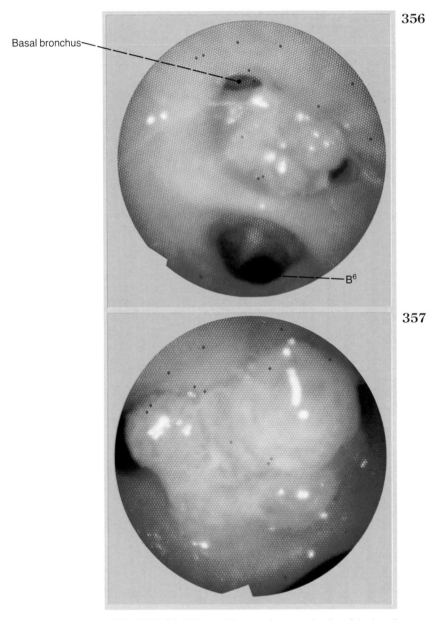

**356, 357** Multiple nodules can be seen in the right basal bronchus. The tumor is made up of multiple smooth surfaced nodules. White material is also present.

*Patient:* 64-year-old male.
*Smoking history:* 10/day, 43 years.
*Family history:* Nothing in particular.
*Past history:* Pulmonary tuberculosis (age 20).
*Reason for detection:* Pharyngeal discomfort and cough developed 3 months previously. Chest radiograph revealed no abnormality, but sputum cytology yielded a diagnosis of squamous cell carcinoma. (*Center for Adult Diseases, Osaka*)

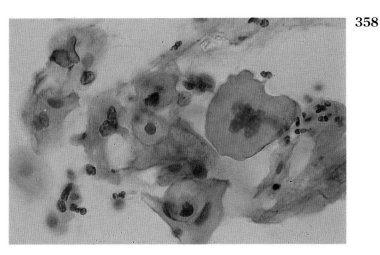

**358** Sputum cytology specimen (×*400*).

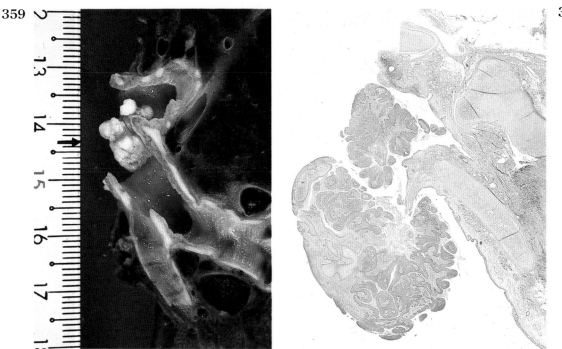

**359, 360** The right lower lobe bronchus seen from the posterior aspect (**359**). Low-power magnification of the orifice of the right lower lobe bronchus shows the tumor protruding as a polyp in the bronchial lumen (**360**).

**POLYPS — 4**

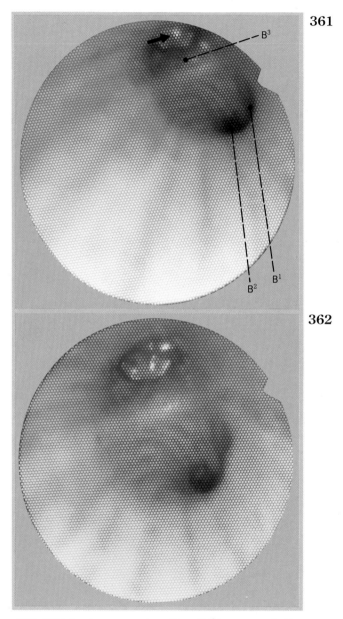

**361, 362** A polyp seen at the orifice of B³ is accompanied by
partial bleeding.

*Patient:* 67-year-old male, self-employed.
*Smoking history:* 40/day, 50 years.
*Family history:* Nothing in particular.
*Reason for detection:* Occasional cough and sputum had developed during the past months and he experienced back pain. Chest radiograph taken by his local physician revealed pneumonia in right $S^3$. Sputum cytology was negative, but as the pneumonia persisted he visited Osaka Adult Diseases Center and fiberoptic bronchoscopy yielded a diagnosis of squamous cell carcinoma. (*Center for Adult Diseases, Osaka*)

**363**

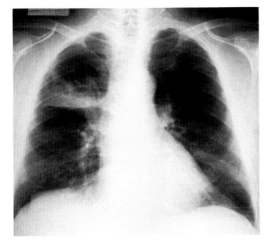

**363** A shadow suggests obstructive pneumonia was limited to $S^3$.

**364**  **365**

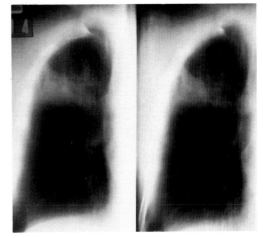

**364, 365** Tomograms demonstrate obstruction of right $B^3$.

**366**

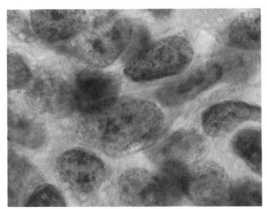

**366** Brushing specimen reveals non-keratinized squamous carcinoma cells (×*1000*).

**367**

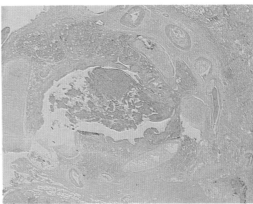

**367** Low-power magnification of a cross-section of right $B^3$ shows the tumor proliferating as a polyp in the bronchial lumen.

**POLYPS – 5**

Middle lobe bronchus

368

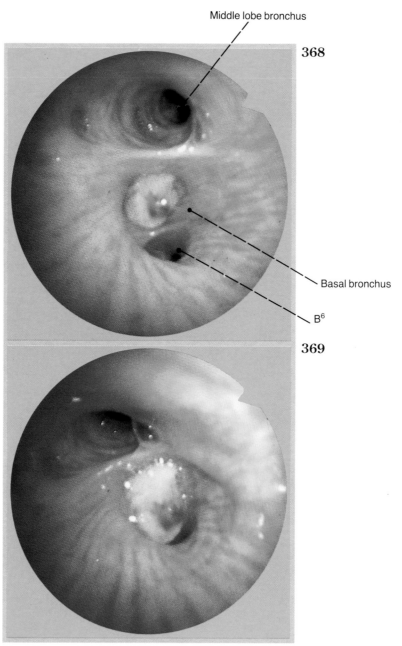

369

Basal bronchus

B⁶

**368, 369** On inspiration the polypoid tumor obstructs the basal bronchus but $B^6$ is patent (**368**). On expiration the polypoid tumor covered with necrotic material is recognized in the lower lobe bronchus but $B^6$ cannot be identified (**369**).

*Patient:* 66-year-old male, teacher.
*Smoking history:* 40/day, 23 years.
*Family history:* Father had gastric cancer.
*Past history:* Diabetes (since age 62).
*Reason for detection:* The patient developed a fever (38°C); 1 month previously an abnormal shadow had been detected on chest radiograph. Antibiotic administration alleviated the fever, but since the abnormal shadow did not disappear the patient came to Osaka Habikino Hospital. Sputum cytology was negative. (*Osaka Habikino Hospital*)

**370**

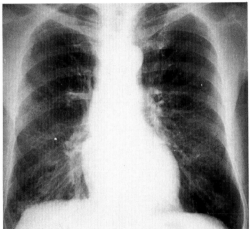

**371**

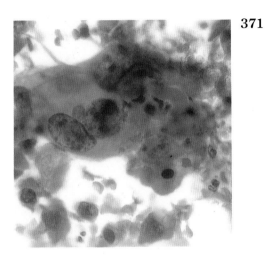

**370** On chest radiograph, a shadow suggestive of pneumonia is recognized in the right lower lung field. Tomogram showed findings of mucoid impaction and decrease in volume of the right lower lobe.

**371** Brushing cytology reveals squamous cell carcinoma (×*400*).

**372**

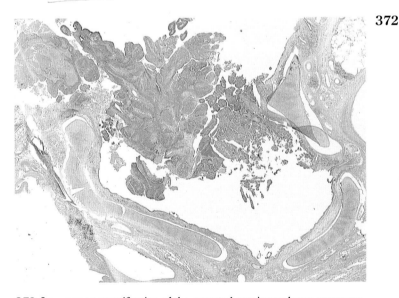

**372** Low-power magnification of the resected specimen shows squamous cell carcinoma in the bronchial lumen.

**POLYPS — 6**

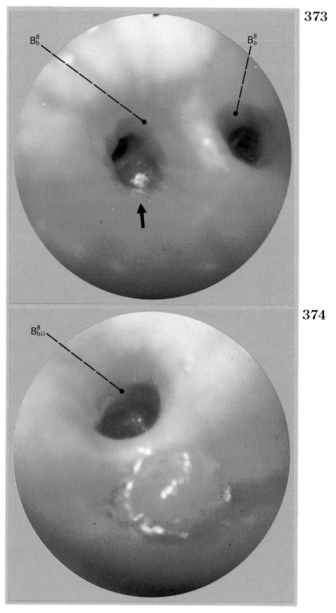

**373**

**374**

**373, 374** A tumor can be seen in the distal portion of right $B_b^8$ (**373**). The polyp can be seen to cause total obstruction in $B_b^8$ (**374**). The surface of the tumor is smooth and glossy.

Patient: 63-year-old male.
Smoking history: 15/day, 38 years.
Past history: Pleurisy (age 20).
Reason for detection: Bloody sputum appeared 3 months previously. Although there was no abnormal shadow on chest radiograph, sputum cytology revealed squamous cell carcinoma. (*Center for Adult Diseases, Osaka*)

**375**

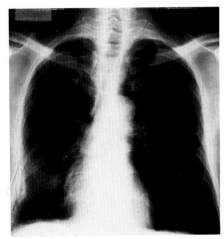

**375** Chest radiograph shows a shadow indicative of old pleurisy, as a result of which the heart shadow is shifted toward the right, but no active lesion appears present.

**376**

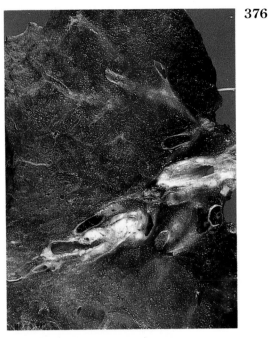

**376** Resected specimen suggests that the lesion originated in $B^8_{bi}$, protruding into the lumen.

**377**

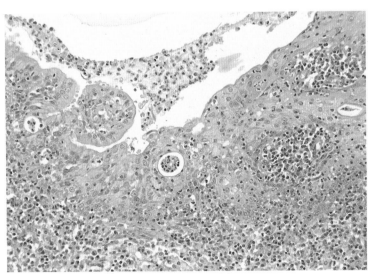

**377** Histological appearance of the tumor demonstrates squamous cell carcinoma ($\times 100$).

## MULTIPLE INCIDENCE – 1

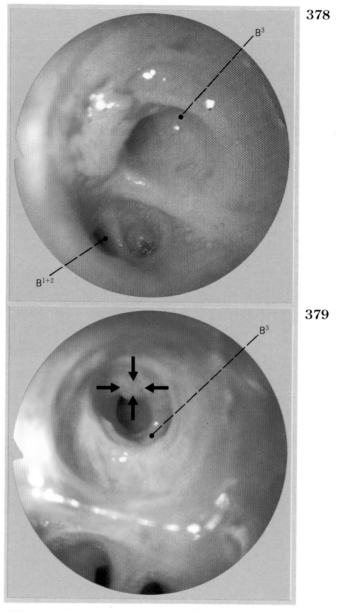

**378, 379** A nodule at the orifice of B$^3$ appears edematous and granular (**378**). A small nodule can be recognized in the distal portion of B$^3$ (**379**).

*Patient:* 71-year-old male, unemployed.
*Smoking history:* 30/day, 50 years.
*Family history:* Nothing in particular.
*Reason for detection:* Squamous cell carcinoma was detected by sputum cytology on a regular checkup. The chest radiograph was normal. (*Tokyo Medical College Hospital*)

**380**

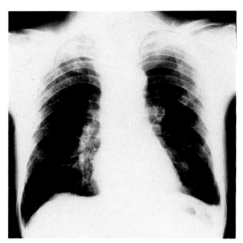

**380** Chest radiograph shows evidence of tumor.

**381**

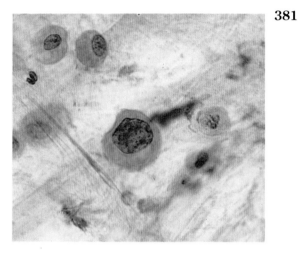

**381** Sputum cytology specimen reveals non-keratinizing squamous carcinoma cells (×*400*).

**382**

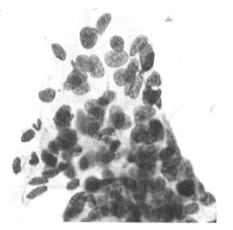

**382** Brushing cytology specimen shows a cluster of non-keratinizing squamous carcinoma cells with increased chromatin (×*400*).

**383**

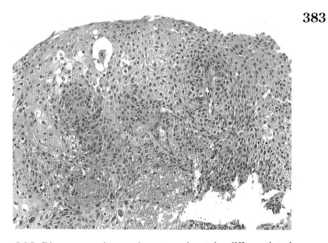

**383** Biopsy specimen shows moderately differentiated squamous cell carcinoma that involves the capillaries in the tumor (×*100*).

## MULTIPLE INCIDENCE — 2

*Patient:* 56-year-old male.
*Smoking history:* 20/day, 38 years.
*Past history:* Nothing in particular.
*Reason for detection:* Bloody sputum had appeared for approximately 1 month. He took part in a mass survey and the sputum cytology results indicated the need for follow-up. Fiberoptic bronchoscopy revealed tumors in the right basal bronchus and lingular bronchus. (*Center for Adult Diseases, Osaka*)

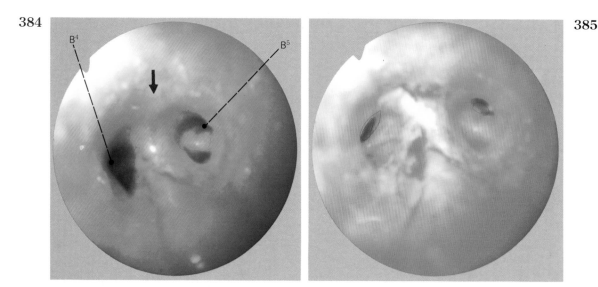

**384** **385**

**384, 385** The bifurcation of B$^4$ and B$^5$ was thickened and bled easily. The mucosal surface was rough and granular, suggesting superficial invasion.

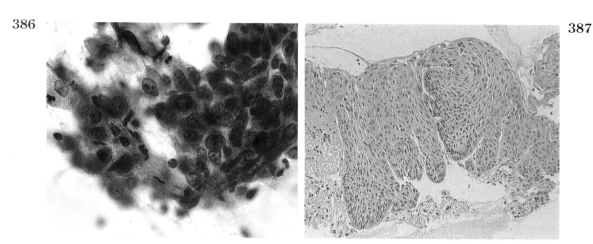

**386** **387**

**386** Brushing cytology specimen from left B$^5$ (×*400*).

**387** Biopsy specimen from the lingular bronchus (×*100*).

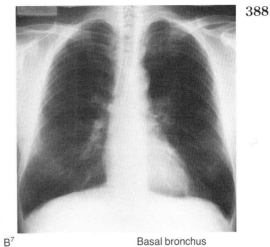

**388**

**388** Chest radiograph shows no abnormal findings.

B⁷

Basal bronchus

**389**

**390**

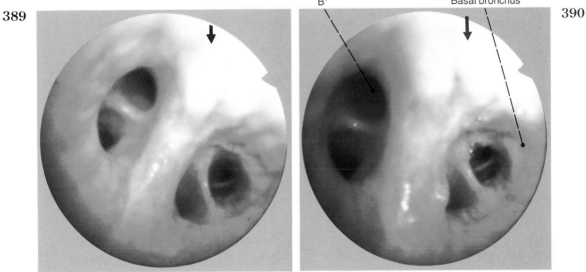

**389, 390** The bifurcation of B⁷ and the basal bronchus is slightly thickened and in addition a nodule can be observed. The tumor surface is irregular.

**391**

**392**

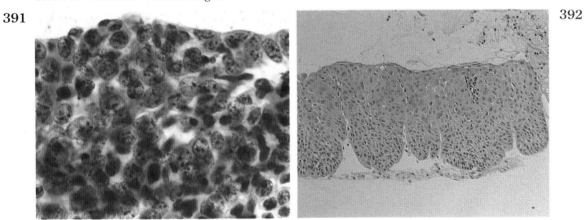

**391** Brushing cytology specimen from right B⁷ (×*400*).

**392** Biopsy specimen from right B⁷ (×*100*).

## MULTIPLE INCIDENCE — 3

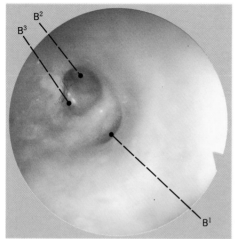

**393** The mucosa of the right upper lobe bronchus shows a mound-like swelling.

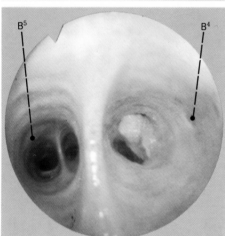

**394** A polypoid lesion can also be seen in right $B_a^4$.

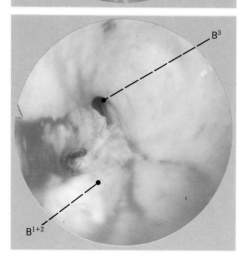

**395** The left upper division bronchus is stenotic due to tumor and submucosal invasion. The orifices of $B^{1+2}$ and $B^3$ can hardly be seen.

*Patient:* 72-year-old male, unemployed.
*Smoking history:* 30/day, 52 years.
*Family history:* Mother died of esophageal carcinoma.
*Past history:* Hypertension (age 50), operation for ileus (age 68).
*Reason for detection:* Cough and bloody sputum appeared 3 months previously and sputum cytology revealed squamous cell carcinoma. Fiberoptic bronchoscopy revealed three tumors and treatment was performed by a combination of photo-dynamic therapy (PDT) and chemotherapy (CDDP+VDS+MMC), resulting in complete response. Clinically, this was a case of synchronous triple lung cancer that was radiologically occult. (*Kinki Central Hospital*)

PDT

**396**

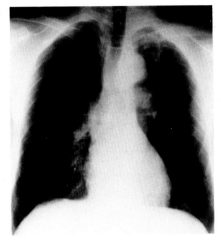

**397**

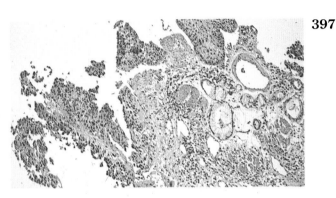

**398**

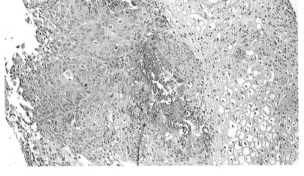

**396** In the left upper lung field a thin-walled tuberculous cavity and cord-like shadow can be seen, which had been pointed out for the previous 10 years.

**397** Biopsy specimen from the right upper lobe bronchus reveals squamous cell carcinoma (×*40*).

**398** Biopsy specimen from right $B_a^4$ shows squamous cell carcinoma (×*40*).

**399** Biopsy specimen from the left upper division bronchus also shows squamous cell carcinoma (×*40*).

**399**

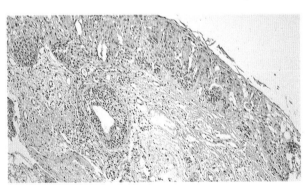

## MULTIPLE INCIDENCE — 4

*Patient:* 63-year-old male, unemployed.
*Smoking history:* 30/day, 42 years.
*Family history:* Father died of hepatocellular carcinoma.
*Past history:* Bronchial asthma (age 26), left epididymitis operation (age 26), appendectomy (age 48).
*Reason for detection:* Sputum cytology, as part of a neighborhood mass survey, revealed squamous cell carcinoma but the chest radiograph was normal. (*Tokyo Medical College Hospital*)

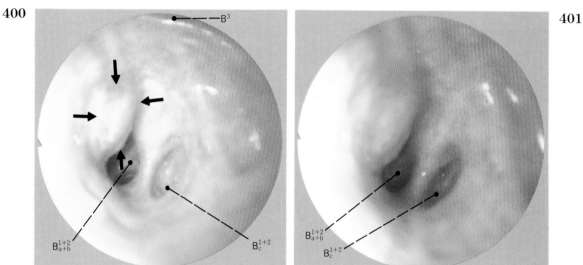

**400**                                                    **401**

**400, 401** Protrusion in $B_{a+b}^{1+2}$, not accompanied by distortion of mucosal folds.

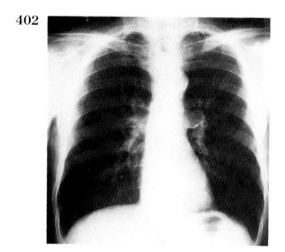

**402** Chest radiograph reveals no abnormality.

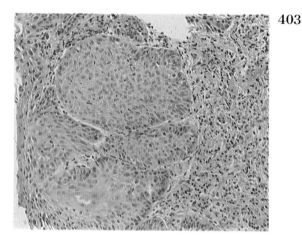

**403** Biopsy specimen shows well-differentiated squamous cell carcinoma, in the lower portion of which an irregular wave-like pattern suggests interstitial invasion.

Reason for detection: After treatment of the left $B^{1+2}$ early stage lesion by PDT the patient was followed up for 5 years, when at age 68 another early stage lesion was detected in left $B^6$. Brushing cytology and biopsy yielded a diagnosis of squamous cell carcinoma.

**404** 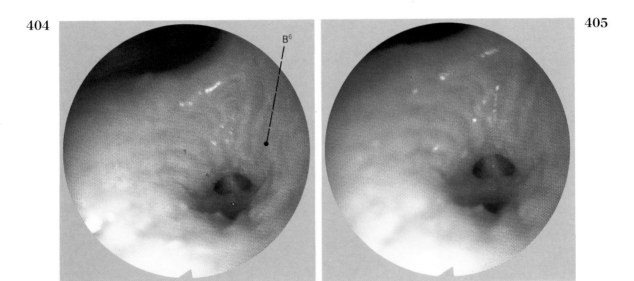 **405**

**404, 405** The mucosa in $B^6$ shows granular irregularity with fusion and distortion of mucosal folds.

**406** 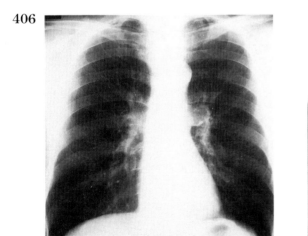 **407**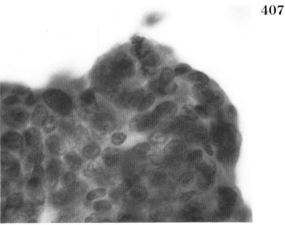

**406** Chest radiograph 5 years after the first lesion was detected shows no abnormality.

**407** Brushing cytology specimen shows a cluster of cells with irregularly sized nuclei and increased chromatin (×400).

# 4 Early Stage Lung Cancer Treatment

The results of the treatment of lung cancer have improved as a result of improvements in diagnostic and therapeutic methods and in pre- and postoperative management. Compared with other stages of lung cancer, results for early stage cases have been particularly encouraging. Looking at the histological type of lung cancer in relation to the site of occurrence, almost all central (hilar) early stage cases are squamous cell carcinomas, whereas most peripheral early stage lung cancers are adenocarcinomas. Depending on the location and histology, the surgical approach can differ, which underlines the importance of classifying lung cancers into central and peripheral lesions.

## PROGRESS IN THE TREATMENT OF EARLY STAGE LUNG CANCER

Surgery has played the principal role in the treatment of lung cancer, and with the development of lung cancer surveys, especially sputum cytology, increasing numbers of central early stage lung cancers are being detected. Most of these tumors are superficial rather than space-occupying lesions. Furthermore, as it is also becoming apparent that cases that develop lung cancer have a tendency to develop multiple lesions we have reached a stage where we must reassess the optimal therapeutic strategies in individual cases. By the end of 1986 a total of 97 cases of early stage lung cancer had been treated at Tokyo Medical College (**Table 9**) by either surgery alone, photodynamic therapy[1-4] (PDT) alone, surgery and combined therapy in addition to PDT, and combined therapy or PDT plus surgery.

Of the total of 46 early stage lung cancers, the 10 cases treated up to 1979 received either surgery or surgery plus combined therapy, but from 1980 onward those methods were the first treatment of choice in only four cases (11.1%), while PDT alone was the first treatment of choice in 12 cases (33.3%) and PDT plus combined therapy (including the above 12) was performed in 14 cases (38.9%), indicating a significant difference in the approach to the treatment of early stage lung cancer.

Combined therapy consisted of chemotherapeutic regimens – such as Mitomycin C (MMC), Adriamycin (ADM), cisplatin (CPA), Carbazilquinone (CQTM), 5-fluorouracil (5-Fu), VCR and, more recently, CDDP and VDS – $^{60}$Co or Lineac radiation, and immunotherapy with BCG cell wall skeleton (BCG-CWS), Nocardia cell wall skeleton (N-CWS), and OK-432.

**Table 9.** Therapeutic strategies in early stage lung cancer (Percent of total inside parentheses)

| | | Number of cases | Surgery alone | Surgery + combined therapy (except PDT) | PDT alone | PDT + surgery | PDT + combined therapy (except surgery) | PDT + surgery + combined therapy |
|---|---|---|---|---|---|---|---|---|
| Central | Up to 1979 | 10 | 6 | 4 | 0 | 0 | 0 | 0 |
| | 1980–1986 | 36 | 3 | 1 | 12 | 13 | 2 | 5 |
| | Subtotal | 46 | 9 (19.6) | 5 (10.9) | 12 (26.1) | 13 (28.3) | 2 (4.3) | 5 (10.9) |
| Peripheral | Up to 1979 | 42 | 15 | 27 | 0 | 0 | 0 | 0 |
| | 1980–1986 | 9 | 3 | 2 | 1 | 1 | 0 | 2 |
| | Subtotal | 51 | 18 (35.3) | 29 (56.9) | 1 (2.0) | 1 (2.0) | 0 | 2 (3.9) |
| Total | | 97 | 27 (27.8) | 34 (35.1) | 13 (13.4) | 14 (14.4) | 2 (2.1) | 7 (7.2) |

**408**

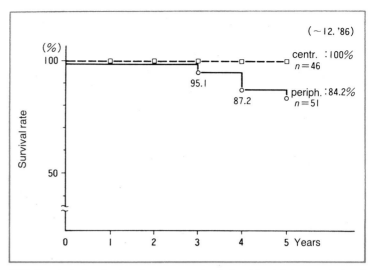

(~12. '86)

**408** Survival of early stage lung cancer: 'centr.' and 'periph.' are central and peripheral lesions, respectively, for five-year period to December 1986.

Excluding deaths due to unrelated causes, as of 1987 the 5-year survival of the 46 central early stage cases (1 adenocarcinoma, 45 squamous cell carcinomas) treated at Tokyo Medical College was 100% (**408**). However, the most recent figures show a decline to 98.3%. According to the report of Naruke[5] the 5-year survival of 290 cases of early stage lung cancer was 80.2% overall (excluding other causes of death) and 80.6% in central early stage cases.

Other causes of death were cancer of other organs (3 cases), pneumonia (3 cases), cardiac infarction, gastric perforation, cardiac insufficiency, and operative death. In particular, in elderly cases pneumonia following pulmonary resection and cardiopulmonary insufficiency due to cardiac infarction represent major hazards.

### SURGICAL TREATMENT
Of the 97 early stage cases of lung cancer treated at Tokyo Medical College, 82 (84.5%) were treated surgically. Of these, 32 were central cases, 28 being treated by lobectomy and 4 by pneumonectomy.

According to a Ministry of Health research group report[5] of 290 resected early stage cases treated between 1972 and 1984, 84 were central lesions, of which 75 underwent lobectomies and 9 underwent pneumonectomies.

Most central early stage cases are squamous cell carcinomas and, in such cases, it is easier to determine the presence or absence of lymph node metastasis than in adenocarcinomas.[6] However, in cases involving main bronchi, in which in the past total pneumonectomies had been performed, the loss of pulmonary function is extremely large. In elderly cases or cases with poor cardiopulmonary function, the effects can lead to a fatal outcome. In order to preserve pulmonary function to some degree, combined bronchoplasty plus lobectomy or lobectomy after PDT[7] have been performed. Thirty-two of the 46 central early stage cases were treated surgically. Of the 4 cases treated by total pneumonectomy at Tokyo Medical College Hospital, 3 were operated on prior to the introduction of PDT in 1980. Furthermore, since it is difficult to preoperatively assess the degree of intramural invasion in the bronchial wall, in principle mediastinal lymph node dissection is carried out in cases treated by lobectomy.

### CHEMOTHERAPY
Chemotherapy and radiotherapy have been used in early stage lung cancer cases in which, for a variety of reasons, surgery is contraindicated. While some of these cases apparently achieve complete remission,[8] the non-surgical treatment of early stage lung cancer has not yet been established.

For lung cancer that develops in large airways, there are some advantages in terms of approach to treatment. Since the lesion can be visualized endoscopically, local treatment is possible and it is relatively easy to evaluate the effects of treatment. In the chemotherapy of early stage lung cancer, various approaches – such as

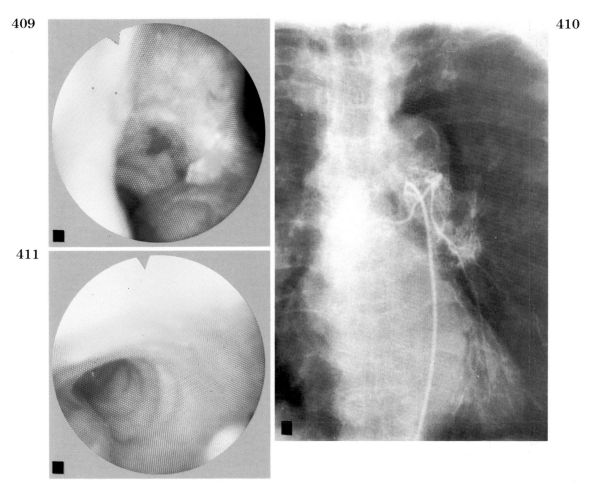

**409–411** Case treated by chemotherapy – 1. A small squamous cell carcinoma was detected in the left main bronchus of a 73-year-old male (**409**); bronchial arteriograph (**410**); after two courses of bronchial artery injection (Mitomycin C, Carbazilquinone) the tumor has disappeared and the mucosa appears almost normal (**411**).

bronchial artery instillation (BAI) – are used to increase the concentration of the drug in the tumor. This technique uses a special injection needle inserted via a fiberoptic bronchoscope, and is mainly employed in protruding lesions originating in large airways, as far as subsegmental bronchi. The drugs employed have primarily been bleomycin and Peplomycin; because only a small amount can be given at a single injection, it is usually necessary to repeat the procedure several times. There have also been reports on the efficiency of injections of immunopotentiators such as Nocardia cell wall skeleton or OK-432.

Direct injection of antitumoral agents via the fiberoptic bronchoscope into the bronchial artery supplying the tumor can result in much higher concentrations of agent in the tumor than would be possible by conventional systemic administration. Drugs employed in this modality include Carbazilquinone, Mitomycin C, Adriamycin and, more recently, cisplatin. A squamous cell carcinoma located at the orifice of the left main bronchus, inoperable because of the location of the tumor and the age of the patient, is shown in **409–411**. Mitomycin C and Carbazilquinone were injected together into the bronchial artery twice. The tumor disappeared completely and the patient has lived for more than 10 years.

Systemic chemotherapy is of course indicated

164

**412** 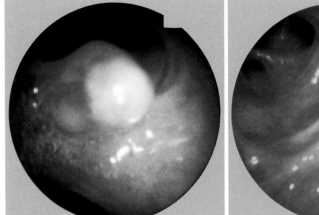 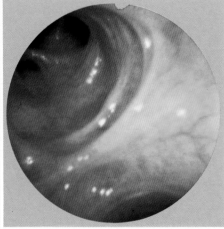 **413**

**412, 413** Case treated by chemotherapy – 2. A protruding lesion was detected at the orifice of left $B^3$ and a polypoid lesion at the orifice of the right lower lobe bronchus in a 72-year-old male. While treating the right lower lobe tumor by radiotherapy, systemic administration of 80 mg/m$^2$ cisplatin was also carried out. The figure shows the tumor in left $B^3$ (**412**). After administration of cisplatin the bifurcation of $B^3$ and the lingular bronchus shows a cicatricial formation (**413**).

in advanced lung cancer cases. Recently, cisplatin has been reported to be effective in non-small cell carcinoma and some investigators anticipate that it could play a role even in cases of early stage cancer. The authors experienced one inoperable case (**412, 413**) in which squamous cell carcinoma was detected simultaneously in both lungs; chemotherapy alone resulted in the disappearance of the tumors and the patient is apparently disease-free more than 3 years later.

However, the reasons for inoperability are usually age or insufficiency of vital organs, such as the lungs, heart, kidneys, and liver; therefore, great care in performing chemotherapy is necessary.

**RADIOTHERAPY**

If a sufficient dose can be delivered, a relatively high rate of local cure can be anticipated. Although opinions vary concerning the dose of radiation required to obtain cure, for early stage lung cancer a dose of at least 60 Gy would appear necessary. In central lung cancer it may be difficult to localize exactly the site of the lesion. Therefore, it is extremely important to accurately

determine the site and extent by fiberoptic bronchoscopy to determine the radiotherapy field. In **414** and **415** a nodular infiltrative type of squamous cell carcinoma at the bifurcation of the left upper division bronchus is shown. Radiotherapy was chosen as the treatment of choice because of advanced age (75 or over), and the patient is healthy 6 years later.

In cases in which radiotherapy is employed as the first treatment of choice, the patient is usually inoperable for the same reasons mentioned at the end of the preceding section on chemotherapy. Thus, attention must be paid to the possibility of side effects, such as lung fibrosis and esophagitis, which can be especially marked when radiotherapy is performed after chemotherapy with Adriamycin, Bleomycin, Peplomycin, and Mitomycin C.

**PDT**

**Photodynamic therapy**

Laser treatment modalities in lung cancer include high-energy laser vaporization and low-energy photodynamic therapy (PDT). In this section we

**414** 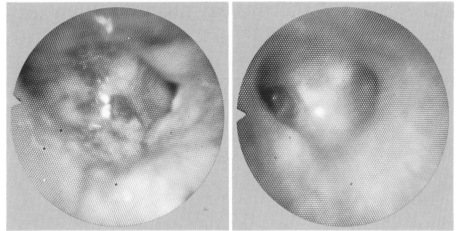 **415**

**414, 415** Case treated by radiotherapy. Nodular invasive-type squamous cell carcinoma developing at the bifurcation of the left upper division bronchus in a 78-year-old male (**414**). After 70 Gy irradiation, the tumor disappeared, leaving only a cicatricial formation. Brushing cytology was negative (**415**).

deal with the PDT, which has obtained encouraging results in early stage cases of cancer, including early stage lung cancer. PDT has attracted attention because of its specificity for malignant tissue.[9,10] This method involves the use of a relatively tumor-specific photosensitizing agent that destroys the tumor with minimal effects on surrounding normal tissue. As shown in **416**, the mechanism of PDT is based on absorption of laser light energy by the photosensitizer, which enters an excited state. In order for the singlet excited photosensitizer to return to its ground state it releases energy, which is transferred to oxygen in the tissue, producing excited-state oxygen. The oxygen in this excited state is considered to be singlet oxygen or a superoxide,[11] and it is this substance that causes the damage and necrosis of the malignant tissue in which it is contained.[12] Obviously, if the photosensitizer has a specific affinity for malignant tissue, it would then be possible to perform specific treatment for malignant tumors.

**416**

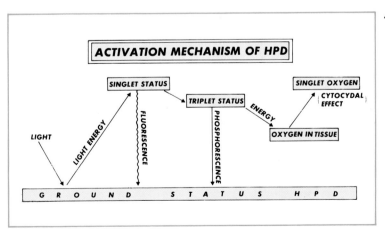

**416** The mechanism of action of PDT.

166

Bis- 1 -[ 8 -( 1 -hydroxyethyl) deuteroporphyrin-3-yl] ethyl ether

**417** Dihematoporphyrin ether (DHE).

### Tumor-specific photosensitizers

Photodynamic therapy began to be employed clinically in the latter half of the 1970s and the photosensitizer used at that time by Dougherty and his colleagues at Roswell Park Memorial Institute was hematoporphyrin derivative (HpD).[13] Uptake of HpD by malignant tissue is 10 times that of normal tissue 2–3 days after administration and induces sensitivity to light.

HpD is obtained by treating hemoglobin with acetic and sulfuric acids. It is sensitive to light and absorbs light most efficiently at a wavelength of approximately 400 nm. The fluorescent red light that it emits on returning to its ground state from the excited singlet state has peaks at 630 and 690 nm.

HpD has affinity for tumor cell cytoplasm and cell membrane.[14] Since it does not have affinity for the cell nucleus, HpD is considered to be safe material, i.e. does not have mutagenic effects. In tissue it is located mostly around blood vessels.

Recently another photosensitizer, a second-generation form of HpD, dihematoporphyrin ether[15] (DHE), (**417**) has been developed which has even higher malignant tissue-specific localization. In addition, photosensitizers containing chlorine or chlorophyll are being developed.

### Treatment equipment and methodology

Lasers employed for this modality include argon dye lasers (**418** and **419**) and gold vapor lasers (**420**). An excited dimer laser system is also being developed; this is discussed in Chapter 2 (see also **45**). Transmission of the laser beam is performed via a 400 μm quartz fiber (Fujikura Electric, Tokyo, Japan), which is inserted through the instrumentation channel. A dose of 2.5–5.0 mg/kg body weight HpD or 2.0 mg/kg DHE is injected intravenously; then, 48–72 h later, the laser photoradiation procedure is performed (**421**). A light density of about 200–400 J/cm$^2$ is desirable. For superficial tumors, the procedure is performed with the tip of the fiber a slight distance from the surface; for protrusive lesions, the tip of the fiber can also be inserted into the lesion for interstitial photoradiation.[16–19]

### Cases treated by PDT

As shown in Table 10, early stage lung cancer cases treated at the Department of Surgery, Tokyo Medical College consisted of 36 lesions in 35 cases. Of these, the histological type was squamous cell carcinoma in 34 cases (35 lesions) and adenocarcinoma in 1 case. Of these, 26 were superficial invasion tumors and 10 were polypoid

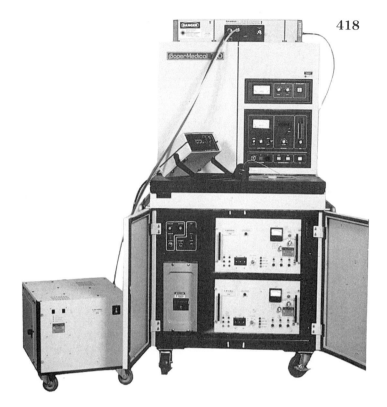

**418** Cooper LaserSonics 770D argon dye laser, wavelength 630 nm.

**419** Fujinon PDT computer-controlled argon dye laser, wavelength 630 nm.

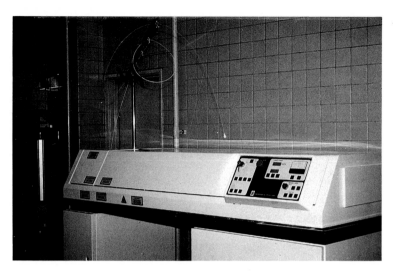

**420** Quentron gold vapor laser, wavelength 628 nm.

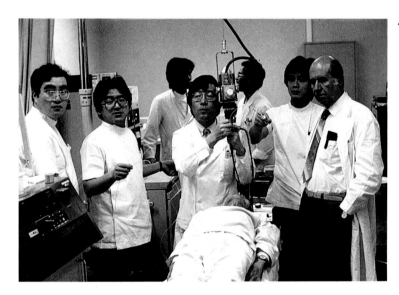

**421** A PDT session.

tumors. Lesions ranged from those within a single bronchus to those extending over several bronchi.

Complete remission was obtained in 74.3% of cases and several have already survived 5 years or more.[20,21] With one exception, all the cases in which complete remission of the tumor was obtained were of limited extent and did not extend beyond a single bronchus. On the other hand, all those cases in which recurrence was observed had extended over more than one bronchus or had extended beyond the bronchial cartilage. This suggests that insufficient therapeutic effects were caused by insufficient laser light delivery, because of the extent or depth of the lesion or because of the difficulties presented in some cases by the anatomical site involved. At present, the conditions under which one can

**Table 10.** Cases in which the endoscopic findings suggested early stage lung cancer (Department of Surgery, Tokyo Medical College, March 31, 1987)

| | |
|---|---|
| Number of cases | 35 (36 lesions) |
| Age distribution | 63–82 |
| Sex | male 34, female 1 |
| Histological type | squamous cell carcinoma 34 (35 lesions) adenocarcinoma 1 (1 lesion) |
| *Endoscopic findings* | |
| Granular surface type | 26 |
| Nodular type | 10 |
| Lesion area | $1 \times 0.5\,cm^2$ to $5.3 \times 2\,cm^2$ |
| Lesion volume | $0.2 \times 0.2 \times 0.2\,cm^3$ to $1 \times 0.5 \times 0.5\,cm^3$ |
| Inoperable | 15 |
| Surgery refused | 7 |
| Surgery after PDT | 13 |

expect to obtain complete remission by PDT are as follows:

- The entire tumor can be visualized endoscopically and photoradiated.
- The lesion is an intraepithelial type limited to the epithelium or within the cartilage layer.
- A small lesion limited to within one bronchus.
- The energy dose should be about $180\,J/cm^2$.

170

422 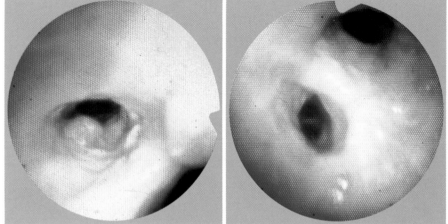 423

**422, 423** Case treated by PDT – 1. An early stage squamous cell lung cancer detected in right $B_b^2$ of a 74-year-old male was the first case of early stage cancer treated by PDT in the world. The lesion is shown before treatment (**422**) and 2 years after treatment (**423**). The patient died of unrelated causes 4 years after treatment. Autopsy revealed no malignant findings.

424 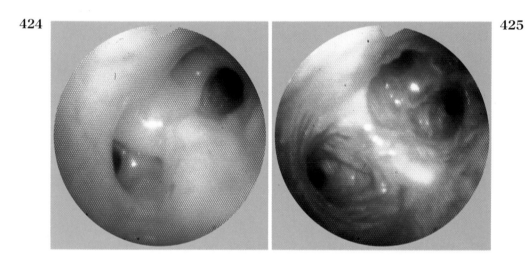 425

**424, 425** Case treated by PDT – 2. Early stage squamous cell lung cancer was detected in the right upper lobe bronchus of a 59-year-old female, based on sputum cytology (**424**). The findings on the second week after treatment show the tumor to have completely disappeared (**425**). This was the first case of cancer to be treated by PDT only in which the patient survived for a further 10 years.

**426**  **427**

**428**  **429**

**430**

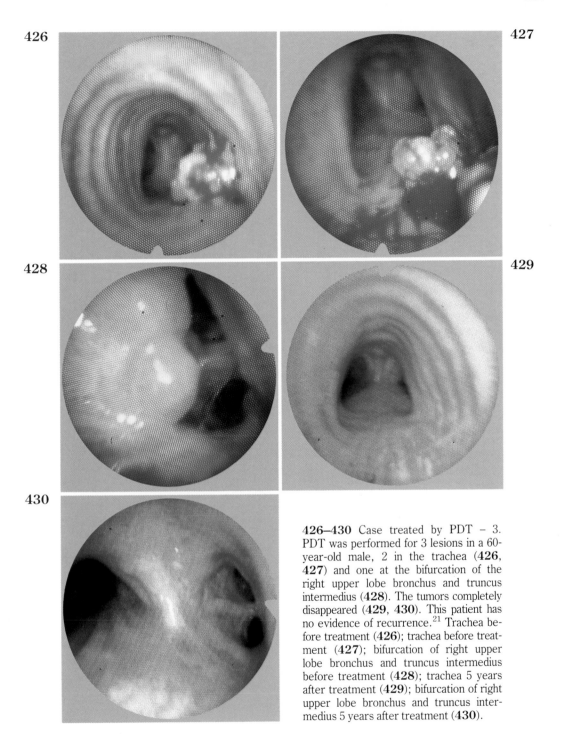

**426–430** Case treated by PDT – 3. PDT was performed for 3 lesions in a 60-year-old male, 2 in the trachea (**426**, **427**) and one at the bifurcation of the right upper lobe bronchus and truncus intermedius (**428**). The tumors completely disappeared (**429**, **430**). This patient has no evidence of recurrence.[21] Trachea before treatment (**426**); trachea before treatment (**427**); bifurcation of right upper lobe bronchus and truncus intermedius before treatment (**428**); trachea 5 years after treatment (**429**); bifurcation of right upper lobe bronchus and truncus intermedius 5 years after treatment (**430**).

**431**

**432**

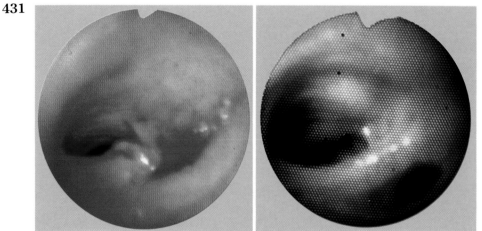

**431, 432** Case treated by PDT – 4. Early stage squamous cell lung cancer located in $B_b^{10}$ in a 76-year-old male with bloody sputum (**431**). Four weeks after treatment, the tumor had totally disappeared (**432**). The patient died due to cerebral infarction 3 years after treatment, but immediately before his death detailed examinations revealed no evidence of recurrence.

**433**

**434**

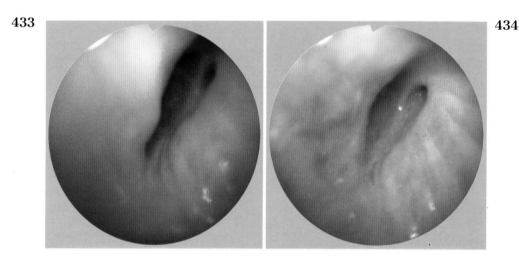

**433, 434** Case treated by PDT – 5. A case of early stage squamous cell lung cancer in the right upper lobe bronchus of a 70-year-old male (**433**). The findings 3 weeks after treatment show the tumor has completely disappeared (**434**), and he has since been apparently disease-free for more than 8 years.

**435** 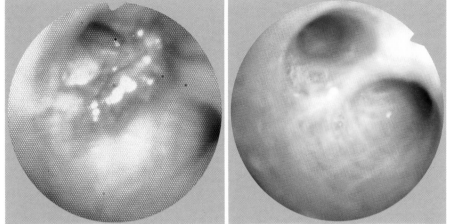 **436**

**435, 436** Case treated by PDT – 6. An early stage squamous cell lung cancer at the bifurcation of right $B^1$ and $B^2$ in a 70-year-old male (**435**). The tumor had disappeared 1 month after treatment (**436**). The man died of unrelated causes 33 months after treatment and there was no evidence of recurrence.

**437** 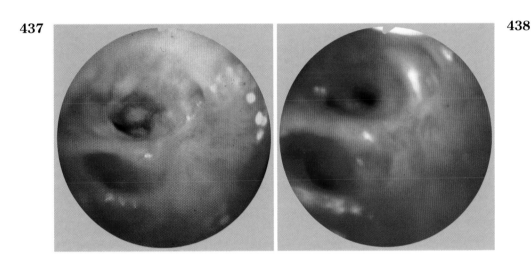 **438**

**437, 438** Case treated by PDT – 7. A granular-type early stage squamous cell lung cancer was detected in $B^{1+2}_{a+b}$ (**437**) in a 62-year-old male and was treated by radiotherapy because of poor pulmonary function; but since recurrence developed, PDT was performed. The photo on the right (**438**), one month after PDT, shows disappearance of the tumor within the visual range of the endoscope. After 16 months the patient succumbed due to poor lung function; an autopsy revealed a tumor in an area peripheral to the treated area, indicating that the laser beam had not penetrated to that area.

174

**439**

**440**

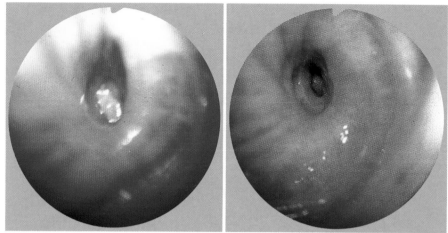

**439, 440** Case treated by PDT – 8. The lesion in this case developed in left B[6] (**439**). The findings show complete disappearance of the tumor after PDT (**440**). The patient is apparently disease-free more than 3 years after treatment.

## REFERENCES

[1]Hayata, Y., Kato, H. *et al.* (1984), Diagnosis and treatment of lung cancer, *Rinsho seijinbyo*, **96**, 2029 (in Japanese).

[2]Hayata, Y. and Kato, H. (1983), Applications of laser photoradiation in the diagnosis and treatment of lung cancer, *JATS*, **3**, 203–210 (in Japanese).

[3]Kato, H. and Konaka, C. (1983), Effectiveness of HpD and radiation therapy in lung cancer, *Porphyrin Photosensitization*, ed. by D. Kessel and T. J. Dougherty, Plenum Press, London, pp. 23–29.

[4]Hayata, Y., Kato, H., *et al.* (1982), Hematoporphyrin derivative and laser photoradiation in the treatment of lung cancer, *Chest*, **81**, 269–277.

[5]Naruke, T. (1985), Clinical features and surgical results of early stage lung cancer, *J. Therapy*, **67**, 1043–1046 (in Japanese).

[6]Ogata, T. (1985), Selection of surgical methods according to the degree of lung cancer progression, *Gekashinryou*, **27**, 17–21 (in Japanese).

[7]Hayata, Y., Kato, H. *et al.* (1984), Hematoporphyrin derivative and photoradiation therapy in early stage lung cancer, *Lasers in Surgery and Medicine*, **4**, 39–47.

[8]Katada, H., Nakamura, S., Horai, T. *et al.* (1980), Combined therapy and cytological findings on inoperable early lung cancer originated from the major bronchus, *Haigan*, **20**, 49–57 (in Japanese).

[9]Dougherty, T. J., Kaufman, J. E. *et al.* (1978), Photoradiation therapy for the treatment of malignant tumors, *Cancer Res.*, **38**, 2628–2635.

[10]Hayata, Y., Kato, H. *et al.* (1982), Hematoporphyrin derivative and laser photoradiation in the treatment of lung cancer, *Chest*, **81**, 269–277.

[11]Sakai, H. (1985), Detection of singlet oxygen from hematoporphyrin derivative (HpD) using luminol, *J. Tokyo Med. Coll.*, **43**, 940–949 (in Japanese).

[12]Kato, H., Aizawa, K. *et al.* (1986), Cytomorphological changes caused by hematoporphyrin derivative and photodynamic therapy, *Lasers in the Life Sciences*, **1**, 13–27.

[13]Lipson, R. L. and Baldes, E. J. (1960), The photodynamic properties of a particular hematoporphyrin derivative, *Arch. Dermatol.*, **82**, 508–516.

[14]Saito, M. (1985), Evaluation of tumor localizing component and intracellular localization site of hematoporphyrin derivative (HpD), *J. Tokyo Med. Coll.*, **43**, 1036–1048 (in Japanese).

[15]Dougherty, T. J., Potter, W. R. *et al.* (1984), The structure of active component of hematoporphyrin derivative. In *Porphyrins in Tumor Phototherapy*, ed. by A. Andreoni and R. Cubbedu. Plenum Press, New York, pp. 23–49.

[16]Kato, H., Konaka, C. *et al.* (1985), Endoskopische Photodynamische Diagnostik und Therapie mit Laser bei Ösophagus-, Magen- und Lungen-Karzinom. *Internist.*, **26**, 675–687.

[17]Kato, H., Konaka, C. *et al.* (1985), Preoperative laser photodynamic therapy in combination with operation in lung cancer. *J. Thorac. Cardiovasc. Surg.*, **90**, 420–429.

[18]Hayata, Y., Kato, H. *et al.* (1986), Cancer treatment by laser. *J. Japan Medical Association.* **96**, 758–762 (in Japanese).

[19]Kato, H., Konaka, C. *et al.* (1987), Photodynamic therapy for lung cancer. *J. Jpn. Bronchoesophagol. Soc.*, **38**, 146–151 (in Japanese).

[20]Kato, H., Konaka, C. *et al.* (1986), Five-year disease-free survival of a lung cancer patient treated only by photodynamic therapy, *Chest*, **90**, 768–770.

[21]Horai, T., Nakamura, S., Nishio, O. *et al.* (1991), A five-year disease-free survivor of multiple unresectable lung cancer treated by photoradiation therapy with haematoporphirin derivative, *Lasers in Medical Science*, in press.

# Index

References in light type are to page numbers, those in **bold** type are to illustrations